T0295641

Explaining Wealth Inequality

This book discusses the origins of wealth inequality and explains how societies can reform to avoid the catastrophe of inequality-induced social breakdown. It develops a theoretical and practical understanding of the principles behind the concept of ownership and property, complete with historical examples.

It proposes a new research perspective focusing on how the problem of wealth concentration is ameliorated by cooperative and collaborative initiatives to enhance the public sphere, without derogating from the private. The book is based on research data compiled from taxation and household data to explore the theme that wealth inequality is made inevitable by possessive behaviour expressed in possessive language. It shows that while inequality is inescapable, we can adopt policies where resources are more efficiently and broadly distributed for public benefit. Such policies are directed towards encouraging voluntary, as opposed to compulsory, wealth transfer to achieve public good.

The primary market for the book consists of academics and students from the fields of economics, including growth and developmental economics, law, sociology, history, business and international trade. It also provides a practical resource for government policy analysts wanting to develop a more detailed understanding of the role played by wealth inequality in a range of social problems.

Benedict Atkinson is a Senior Lecturer in Law at the School of Business, James Cook University Singapore.

Routledge Frontiers of Political Economy

For more information about this series, please visit: www.routledge.com/Routledge-Frontiers-of-Political-Economy/book-series/SE0345

Explaining Wealth Inequality

Property, Possession and Policy Reform

Benedict Atkinson

LONDON AND NEW YORK

First published 2022
by Routledge
2 Park Square, Milton Park, Abingdon, Oxon OX14 4RN

and by Routledge
605 Third Avenue, New York, NY 10158

Routledge is an imprint of the Taylor & Francis Group, an informa business

© 2022 Benedict Atkinson

British Library Cataloguing-in-Publication Data
A catalogue record for this book is available from the British Library

Library of Congress Cataloging-in-Publication Data
Names: Atkinson, Benedict A. C., author.
Title: Explaining wealth inequality: property, possession and policy reform/ Benedict Atkinson.
Description: Abingdon, Oxon; New York, NY: Routledge, 2022. |
Series: Routledge frontiers of political economy | Includes bibliographical references and index.
Identifiers: LCCN 2021022151 (print) | LCCN 2021022152 (ebook) |
ISBN 9781032037363 (hardback) | ISBN 9781032037387 (paperback) |
ISBN 9781003188766 (ebook)
Subjects: LCSH: Wealth–Moral and ethical aspects. | Income distribution. |
Equality–Economic aspects.
Classification: LCC HB251 .A85 2022 (print) | LCC HB251 (ebook) |
DDC 330.1/6–dc23
LC record available at https://lccn.loc.gov/2021022151
LC ebook record available at https://lccn.loc.gov/2021022152

ISBN: 978-1-032-03736-3 (hbk)
ISBN: 978-1-032-03738-7 (pbk)
ISBN: 978-1-003-18876-6 (ebk)

DOI: 10.4324/9781003188766

Typeset in Times New Roman
by Deanta Global Publishing Services, Chennai, India

Contents

Part I
Possession and property

1   Language and possession

Language predisposes humans to a possessive mentality. Settled peoples make sense of surrounding phenomena by acts of notional and then physical annexation. Their innate grammar ensures that they cannot do otherwise. Possessive language leads to possessive thought which leads to possessive action. Possessiveness causes division, because a thing is owned exclusively, with the result that the owner excludes the trespasser from the thing. From exclusion comes social inequality.

Possessiveness is pre-determined by language

In 1957, Noam Chomsky, then at the beginning of his career in linguistics, published a book called *Syntactic Structures,* a 'theory of linguistic structure' which introduced the idea that knowledge of grammar is inborn. The book transformed the study of language structure and acquisition. Few academic fields are as contested as that of linguistics, and Chomsky's language theories are rejected by many linguists. However, many acknowledge Chomsky's profound effect on language theory.[1] His theory of *innate grammar* provides us with many clues as to why humans think possessively and, wherever they gather in settled societies, create property systems.

Chomsky argues that the speed and facility with which children acquire complex grammar disproves the claim that language is acquired from the linguistic cues of parents and others. In a short period of time, a child's linguistic competence vastly outstrips whatever language adults could teach the child in that time (Berwick and Chomsky, 2016).

To demonstrate his argument, Chomsky referred to recursiveness in language. Our grammar is recursive, or generative, meaning that we are linguistically capable of constructing an infinity of sentences. Our linguistic super-capacity is a property of our brain. Grammar, a system of categories and rules that make meaningful communication possible, is the product of a code written into a computer, the brain. Stimuli activate the code.

DOI: 10.4324/9781003188766-1

Chomsky's theory of innate grammar, or what he used to call universal grammar – because language capacity is common to all people – helps to explain how our grammar directs the choices we make to create property, and, more specifically, to seek control by appropriation. Applying the theory of innate or universal grammar, we can say that humans acquire language in the same way, and communicate using similar grammars. Grammars are not identical. All, however, categorise reality in the same way. That is, their modes of classifying phenomena, and explaining human interaction with those phenomena, are the same.

If we examine the possessive case in language, we can identify a common human attitude to the act of possession, which is the condition precedent for creating property. As our grammar shows, humans cannot make sense of the world without asserting possession in myriad ways – I possess my coat, declaring my right to control the custody of the coat, when I say, 'It's my coat'; similarly, I propose that another person possesses a dog when I say, 'You have a friendly dog.'

The possessive case, involving conceptual appropriation, is part of the languages of settled (as opposed to nomadic) peoples. The purpose of the possessive case is to allocate control. Its existence in language tells us that for millennia human forebears recognised that social efficacy requires humans to exercise control – over themselves, over others and over things. The existence of possessive grammar also foretells conflict. If two people say of the same thing, 'It's mine', then antithesis is created, and if dispute follows, an ultimate consequence of dispute may be warfare.

The urge to possess, as Jean-Jacques Rousseau pointed out (1755), is the beginning of conflict. Settled society, according to Rousseau, is disastrous to human happiness. The disaster is one of recognition. Humans recognise the surrounding world and the part that they play in that world. If we borrow from Sartre, who wrote two hundred years after Rousseau, we can interpret Rousseau to say that on leaving the state of nature, humans beheld the Other (Sartre, [1943] 2020). Like Adam and Eve cast out from Eden, they perceived their nakedness. Comparison between self and other began. Then, according to Rousseau, occurred the greatest disaster:

> The first person who, having enclosed a plot of land, took it into his head to say this is mine and found people simple enough to believe him was the true founder of civil society. What crimes, wars, murders, what miseries and horrors would the human race have been spared, had some one pulled up the stakes or filled in the ditch and cried out to his fellow men: Do not listen to this imposter. You are lost if you forget that the fruits of the earth belong to all and the earth to no one!
>
> (1755: Second Part Para 1)

This vivid statement contains a clue about the origin of social inequality. The clue is the word 'mine'. Any personal pronoun claiming possession is at the beginning of a chain of causation that ends in inequality. If something is mine, I must *possess* it. To own something, we must *possess* the thing. Most people think of possession as physical custody of a thing, or at least the legal right to physical custody of the thing. However, possession is notional, not physical. It is impossible to possess a field, a house or a car physically. One can only possess these things mentally, meaning one *apprehends* a field, house or car. What is understood or apprehended mentally is defined as a field, house or car and becomes a legal object that can be sold or leased because it is owned.

The anarchist Pierre-Joseph Proudhon asked the question, 'What is property?' and famously answered that 'It is theft!' (1840: 1). Proudhon did not mean to say that owners are thieves. He meant that a property system dispossesses. If we create property, the owner possesses and others are excluded. These others are, in effect, dispossessed, although the act of possession is not necessarily a direct act of dispossession. The social effect of dispossession is radical. It creates the categories of haves and have-nots. Proudhon thus follows the thought of Rousseau, who warned that social division is begun by dispossession, and maintained by the dichotomous actions of dispossession and possession.

Self and possession

It is important to understand why the dichotomy between possession and non-possession (or indeed dispossession) is born and the social fissure increases. Possession is linked to self. Each person understands external phenomena through the agency of self. Unless I am self-conscious, I am language-incapable. I begin to make sense of my environment and communicate in meaningful language when self and grammar correlate, identifying to every human a world of form, substance, agency and motion.

We describe the world to ourselves and others by using both pronouns of self and pronouns connecting-to-self – *I, me, my, mine, you, yours, his, hers, hers, its, theirs, ours*. Pronouns are the identifiers of self, or objects perceived by the self. *I* have blue eyes. *She* is intelligent. *His* name is Robert. *My* mother was kind. *Our* team will win. *They* are from Spain. *Her* house is bigger than *your* house.

The self is unique and its essence incommunicable. We *share* thoughts and feelings, but a person's experience of self, a person's selfhood, is unknowable to another person. Our apartness is the beginning of property, as we can see from observing the way that we deploy possessive pronouns. The possessive pronouns *possess*. That is *my* house and not *your* house.

This is *our* land and not *yours*. I will drive *my* car to the office. *Our* children are playing. If something is mine, it is not yours. An assertion of possession may be uncontroversial. Alternatively, it may be contested. It may elicit inimical emotion.

Possession occurs in many ways. I possess my body and its parts inalienably, but my possession of my car is alienable. My arm is connected to my self. My car is not. I can sell my car. I cannot sell my arm. People claim to possess their children as theirs, though not inalienably, since as well as being 'our' children, they are themselves. Two verbs, 'have' and 'belong', perform a coadjutant function expanding the range of descriptive possessive statements in a way that pronouns and adjectives cannot ('You may have that coat'; 'I do not belong here').

The idea of control expressed in pronouns and adjectives, and the verb representations of possession, distil in the language patterns of every linguistically capable person a dialectic of appropriation (mine) and contest or antithesis (mine/yours). Possessive grammar is the instrument, and proof, of invariable appropriation. Alienably or inalienably, we declare things (called nouns) to be our property: 'my heart', 'my wife', 'my house'.

Humans can only understand what is external through the agency of self, and the self can only comprehend existence by relating the components of existence to self. It relates by possession. Thus my car belongs to my self, and our house belongs to my self *and* a class related to my self, whereas your car belongs to your self because it does not belong to my self. Self is the determiner of possessive grammar. If we accept Chomsky's theory, we can say that our language faculty causes humans to relate things to self and define things as possessable.

This proposition is not contradicted by the existence of social systems that eschewed or eschew property: collectivism in the 20th century, or the peripatetic kinship systems of nomadic tribes. A principal reason for collectivism's failure is that it suppressed self-determination, which includes the determination to possess. Among peripatetic peoples, the creation of territory, and kinship relations within the territory, satisfy the self-urge for possession.

Social consequences of possessive grammar

Possessive grammar assigns relational control to a person or thing. The social consequence of our innate tendency to make sense of surrounding matter by mentally defining and possessing that matter is the creation of property systems. People define and appropriate their surroundings, and then distribute control or ownership. Socially, they are perhaps unable to do other than create property systems. Property laws assimilate concepts of possession, occupancy, property and ownership, and cognate ideas of domination, control and wealth.

The act of creating property systems, however, is neither politically nor socially neutral. If people, guided by a mental formulary system that causes them to appropriate external phenomena, assert exclusive rights over land and things, a risk of conflict arises. The history of the world, reduced to its essence, is a contest for land and resources. Possession means dispossession, or more accurately, exclusion. One possesses; the other is excluded. One owns; the other is, potentially, a trespasser.

Possession begins as a mental declaration, and because we possess exclusively, the consequences of our declared possession can destroy the happiness and welfare of individuals and people. The potentially malign consequence of claiming ownership, even metaphorically, can be seen in a passage from Act III Scene II of Shakespeare's play *The Taming of the Shrew*. Petruchio compares his new wife Kate, the 'shrew' of the play's title, to chattels, house, field and so on, which constitute her dowry:

> But for my bonny Kate, she must with me.
> Nay, look not big, nor stamp, nor stare, nor fret;
> I will be master of what is mine own.
> She is my goods, my chattels; she is my house,
> My household stuff, my field, my barn,
> My horse, my ox, my ass, my anything.
> And here she stands, touch her whoever dare.
> I'll bring mine action on the proudest he
> That stops my way in Padua.

Petruchio's conflation of Kate and chattels tells us about mental appropriation and the creation of property. For Petruchio, his self is sovereign. From his speech, we might think that he thinks Kate is indivisible from her dowry. By notionally declaring his wife and her property inseparable, and claiming what is hers as his, he claims to own his wife as well as her property.

Petruchio's liberal use of the personal pronoun betrays his avarice and presumption (although the speech could also be interpreted as a devotional declaration that what is Petruchio's is Kate's also, or that Kate is more important to Petruchio than anything he possesses). What is most noteworthy about the speech, however, is that its possessive claims are not much different from those we make in everyday discourse. Men do not today usually explicitly declare that their wives and their wives' property are their property. But we rarely speak a sentence without making a possessive claim, usually stated by reference to self – I, me, my, mine, our, ours.

Property arrangements are affected by social mores. If Petruchio and Kate married today, Kate would not provide a dowry, and should she inherit property, no law would immediately require her to share that property with Petruchio. However, the principle of property has not altered. Property vests in a person a right of exclusive possession or control, to do with it, within the law, what the owner wishes. We can see that that right, once declared and contested, is a source of perpetual conflict. Our speech invariably and profusely contains possessive assertions that express assumptions about control. If those claims and assumptions are challenged, contest begins and from contest emerges sovereignty.

Contest for sovereignty

Various theories and studies of human behaviour confirm what most people probably regard as self-evident: while humans can join together in society and co-operate with one another to develop and improve their societies, they yet seem innately disposed towards aggression, and will organise to secure the advantage of one group over another. None of these behavioural characteristics tell us much about the origins of social inequality. We can deduce only that people act socially and anti-socially, co-operatively and non-co-operatively.

A possessive mentality is not inescapable. People act co-operatively and create societies that function because of co-operation. They also try assiduously to gain special benefit for themselves. No behavioural studies say that, as a rule, humans want to share equally in benefit. Hierarchy is universal in human societies. In every society, some receive more and some less. Acknowledging these apparent truths, we can say that social inequality is a by-product of the human tendency to seek private advantage. This observation takes account of differences in intellectual and temperamental capability, social circumstances and social support. The advantages conferred on some people by nature and nurture help them, if they are so minded, to secure material advantage for themselves that people less endowed may be unable to attain. From the struggle for advantage emerges status and hierarchy.

Note

1   Criticism of Chomsky's theory of innate or universal grammar is focused on the issues of non-proof and the fact of complex differing forms of grammar and mode of grammar acquisition. Most recently, the linguist Daniel Everett has cited the Piraha language as one that does not show the recursive properties which Chomsky attributes to language.

2   Grammar and property systems

People contest for sovereignty of things: the winners of the contest possess things and the losers are excluded from possession. People co-operate but usually within groups. Possessiveness is native to humans but the contest for possession, which confers more benefits on some and disfavours others, leads to the creation of hierarchies that are anti-social in effect.

Antithesis

Thorstein Veblen (1899) argued that social hierarchy is an instrument of control, maintained by 'force and fraud'. He was not concerned with the social utility, and even necessity, of hierarchy. Veblen coined the term 'conspicuous consumption' to explain the behaviour of rich Americans who displayed themselves to others by expenditure on unnecessary or surplus things – consumer goods, houses, yachts, expensive cars and so on. Their motive, according to Veblen, was to parade uselessness as an artefact of power. He observed that the wealthy class – which he called the 'leisure class' – has throughout history advertised its social uselessness as the mark of its supremacy. Leisured people, unlike others, can afford leisure, and their leisure is socially approved. They, unlike others, can afford to engage in grotesque expenditure on things that they may never use or occupy.

Why hierarchy and unequal distribution rather than co-operation and sharing? Certainly, people co-operate but they tend to do so within groups. German idealist philosophers tried hard to understand the secret of social process. The idealists devised a causal triptych which Marx (1873) turned into his theory of history: history is made by the action of thesis, antithesis and finally synthesis.

The idea of antithesis is consistent with what is known of animal behaviour. Animals, including humans, are territorial, and do not welcome incursions into their territory. In the case of humans, language helps to transform the territorial instinct. We are creatures of volition and intention, and we can

DOI: 10.4324/9781003188766-2

say, 'I want that', or 'I need to own that', or 'I'm going to take that thing from you.'

We can call any of these three statements a thesis. What is more critical in the passage of history is antithesis. The possessor of whatever thing or item people 'want', 'need' or intend to 'take' is likely to reject possessive assertions. Antithesis, at least in this example, leads to conflict. If we want to call the outcome of conflict synthesis, then synthesis follows antithesis, because conflict resolves in some outcome, even though its ending may signify the beginning of new claims, contests and presumptive 'synthesis'.

Prisoners of possessiveness

More importantly, humans are, to some extent, prisoners of their possessive grammar. People know no other way than to make notional annexations of what is around them. They self-apprehend sentience, materiality, motion, time, wish and memory, and the self declares, 'I possess' *or* 'some other – other than my self – possesses'. We cannot avoid declaring possessive affiliation. By saying 'my mother', I notionally annex my mother to me. I could instead say, 'this is the woman who says she is my mother', or 'this is the woman who gave birth to me'. Both circumlocutions still involve notional annexation of a person who is *mine – my* mother. As soon as I declare consanguinity I acknowledge that no other person can be my mother.

My notional annexation excludes anyone other than siblings from the category of maternal possession. Likewise, if I say, 'I like your house', I notionally annex your house to you, and exclude from your possession of your house any other person. What if a person says to me, 'She's not your mother, she's my mother'? What if I say to you, 'I like your house, and I've decided to become the owner of your house'? In these cases, antithesis arises. Dispute is likely to follow. The subject of dispute is *possession*, and our grammar leads us into dispute, whether our possessive statements are direct or indirect.

Plato, writing in the period between 388 and 367 BC, explained how possessive contest over things leads to social conflict:

> Such differences commonly originate in a disagreement about the use of the terms 'mine' and 'not mine', 'his' and 'not his.' ... And is not that the best-ordered State in which the greatest number of persons apply the terms 'mine' and 'not mine' in the same way to the same thing?
> ([c 367 BC] 2007: Bk V)

St John Chrysostom, one of the Church Fathers, referred to 'the very mentioning of the metallic words "mine" and "thine"' when 'all vileness began' ([c 386–398 AD] 1950–1952).

Our possessive mentality, expressed in our language, foments antithesis. It causes us to view the world possessively, and to make possessive claims that may be neutral in effect, or may cause conflict. A reference to 'my mother' is unlikely to be contested. But on a larger scale, possessive claims are likely to be political, and to be opposed politically. Since the beginning of recorded history, groups have fought for *our* land that is said to belong to *our* people. In small and large things, people, seeking to control what surrounds them, assert sovereignty over things, and, if opposed, contest for sovereignty. In larger things, such as the politics of government, the contest for sovereignty results *in* sovereignty: a person or groups secure control over the thing contested.

The result of contest is property systems

Thesis confronted by antithesis, according to idealist theory, leads to synthesis. Alternatively, sovereignty is contested, leading to sovereignty. The practical meaning of these formulations is that synthesis or sovereignty, the way that political power is allocated, is represented by property systems. The word 'property' derives from the Latin *proprius*, or 'one's own'. The noun 'possession' derives from the Latin verb *possidere*, 'to control or occupy', the past participle referring to the act or fact of possessing, or 'to seize upon'. *Possidere* comes from *potis* ('able') and *sedeō* ('sit'). 'Able to sit' or 'sittable' are terms metaphorically apposite to the task of conveying what is meant by the word 'possession': feet planted, the possessor claims by the act of sitting or squatting, control or lordship over whatever is, by this act, declared possessed.

One consequence of exclusive possession is exclusion. People contest for sovereignty of things: the winners of the contest possess things and the losers are excluded from possession. The contest for sovereignty over things material and abstract occurs every day in numberless ways in all parts of social life. When contest for sovereignty concerns control over resources, or access to resources, the outcome of competition creates a system that is a network of things owned and a distributive instrument, allocating benefit and preferment. That system is the property system.

A property system expresses power distribution. Instrumentally, a property system distributes benefit and effects social exclusion, by this means causing social inequality. The property system declares who has, and who does not; who possesses and who does not. The process of inclusion and exclusion is impersonal, though it protects historical political and social settlements that, unless interrupted, continue indefinitely to direct distribution of social benefit in favour of some groups and not others.

A property system evolves. The search for sovereignty continues over time. For instance, the contests for sovereignty that created the modern

British property systems began after the Norman invasion, continued in the long history of feudalism, caused its replacement by a new form of tenure favouring the new rich, and precipitated the long socio-political march to complete suffrage and freehold – the hallmarks, supposedly, of a liberal self-determining society.

At any stage of their evolution, the property systems of Britain have also functioned as instruments of social exclusion, granting more power to the coteries controlling land and enterprise. The exclusionary power made possible by the institution of property may be a bulwark of liberty, permitting exchange (markets) and privacy (for instance, the right to quiet enjoyment of one's house). But if the owner possesses the means of sustenance or survival unavailable to the trespasser, the trespasser may starve.

CASE STUDY: SOLON AND LYCURGUS

The Attic crisis

A famous example of a social crisis is that which resulted in the legal reforms of the Athenian nobleman Solon, who lived from about 640 BC to 559 BC. We know that in Solon's lifetime, a land struggle plagued the societies of Athens and Attica, the region surrounding, and affiliated to, Athens. The struggle illustrates how property or *control* systems, which distribute advantage and disadvantage in society, and which must be understood to function simultaneously as systems of politics, economics, culture and social action, arise from a *contest for sovereignty*.

The Attic crisis that Solon partly resolved arose from such a contest, in this case between social classes. Contest of classes recurs in history. It is unsurprising to discover that contest and crisis in our era, as in that of Solon, usually involves proprietary claims. In the present, globalism, unrestricted movement of capital and people, corporate autonomy and unmediated economic bargaining have all produced for certain classes disproportionate benefit. Other classes have received little or no benefit. Many people have surrendered benefit. The aristocrats of Athens, in the time of Solon, had also procured disproportionate social benefit. Benefit for them impoverished others so greatly that some were compelled to become slaves because they could not pay debts.

As millions today are deprived of legal protection against the imposition of settlements that reduce them to economic servility, so in Solon's era the propertied rich, by exercising superior bargaining power, reduced the less propertied (or propertyless) to indigence – or slavery. As we shall see, a similar social struggle polluted the 500-year history of the Roman republic and resulted in civil war, social ruin and government by autocrats – the emperors.

Solon became known to Athenians as a poet. His patriotic verse encouraged the Athenians to continue their ultimately successful fight against Megara for the island of Salamis. The Athenians gained control of Salamis in approximately 600 BC, when Solon was about 40 years of age. In 594 BC, they, or rather the aristocrats and the people, then on the brink of civil war, agreed that he should be appointed *archon*, chief magistrate or lawmaker, in Athens.

In Solon's lifetime, an economic revolution transformed Attic society. Big landowners abandoned the traditional compact between rich and poor, which had enabled the latter to own and cultivate smallholdings undisturbed by the owners of Attica's large estates. In return for the consent of the people (or *demos*) to the continued political supremacy of the larger landholders, the landed class, numbering many aristocrats, had traditionally refrained from seeking to acquire the land of small farmers. The rich also made a kind of public social provision by refraining from increasing rents excessively, and by refraining from forcing small farmers from their land through competition.

As Solon grew up, the aristocrats began to repudiate arrangements that had for generations maintained social peace in Attica. The change arose for a simple reason: the landed class wished to grow richer. Import of luxuries caused demand for the supply of more luxuries, and the big landowners solved the problem of paying for the new trade by embarking on economic revolution. They enlarged their holdings, often by appropriating public land and buying the land of bankrupt small farmers. Frequently, they forced bankruptcy by refusing to continue credit to farmers approaching – or in – default. Their swollen estates concentrated on production of cereals, especially corn and barley. The big owners employed some propertyless farmers as labourers. Others permitted labourers to occupy land as tenants obliged to donate most of their crops to their landlords. The most unfortunate, the bankrupt, unable to make restitution, might be sold as slaves, or become slave workers on the estates of creditors.

Solon instituted reform, beginning about 594 BC. He resolved the social crisis by cancelling debts and forbidding slavery, but he did not redistribute any of the landholdings of the rich, as many of the poor had hoped. Solon forbade export of produce other than olive oil, by this measure depriving the wealthy of incentive to concentrate on the diversified production for export that had fed a jump in profits, and fuelled their desire to incorporate smallholdings in larger estates.

Separately, he abolished most of the draconian laws (so named after Draco, their author) and remade Athens's system of government. Hitherto, a council of aristocrats had appointed a government of other aristocrats. Now Solon provided for an assembly of four classes, divided according to wealth. Landholders who produced 500 bushels or more of cereals per annum qualified for the highest class, those who produced 300–500 bushels the next class, and those who produced 200–500 bushels the third class. Producers of under 200 bushels, the *thetes,* qualified for the lowest class.

Aristocrats especially, and the unennobled rich, continued to monopolise executive government, since they monopolised the council of state and also controlled the drafting of legislation. The poorer in society acquired some suffrage and some political rights, although the poorest, those who did not own, remained politically and socially disfavoured.

In a rudimentary way, Solon's reforms anticipated the Athenian quasi-plebiscitary democracy that emerged several years after Cleisthenes established the equal right of male citizens to debate legislation (508 BC) – more than 50 years after Solon's death. This democracy, in its unexpurgated form, did not outlive the Peloponnesian War, which ended in Sparta's defeat of Athens in 404 BC. But its existence demonstrated that to some extent the distribution of power, and social arrangements that concentrate possession in the hands of a few, are mutable.

Solon hindered as well as helped the growth of democracy. By concentrating executive power in the hands of the wealthy, and by circumscribing the legislative influence of the less wealthy, he reinforced the idea that power and wealth are properly conjoined, an idea from which his political successors did not depart. His unwillingness to disturb the land monopoly of the rich hardened the conviction of future Athenian politicians that the wealthy and powerful should determine the policy of the city-state and the rights of its inhabitants.

On the other hand, by leaving monopoly untouched and instead trying to reduce the coercive power of the wealthy, Solon established the model for successful land reform. The creation of property classes entitled to certain rights, and the guarantee of tenure of smallholdings, enabled citizens, the *polis*, to negotiate over time more equal distribution of power – a negotiation that resulted in democracy. Democracy proved unstable, however. A system of voting by raised hands, without further ado, resulted in the passing of ill-considered or sometimes maliciously intended motions. Democracy also failed signally to solve the problem of wealth disparity, an enduring cause of disharmony that Solon only partially resolved.

The lesson of Solon

In the present day, the most important lesson of Solon's reforms, supported by many other historical precedents, is that successful alteration of property relations is scarcely achievable by forced redistribution. Property relations are indistinguishable from constitutional or political arrangements. The deciders of constitutions and the controllers of government are members of a propertied class that refuses the compulsory transfer of ownership of land or other things owned. Historically, the only kind of compulsory redistribution that appears to be successful is that which increases the holdings of the main property class. The Crown's expropriation of Church land and its transfer of that property to the new magnates of Reformation England is an example of successful redistribution making the rich richer.

By declining to redistribute land, Solon avoided a socially destructive challenge from the wealthy, who, economically advantaged by his political quiescence, could not legitimately challenge his reforms. Those reforms, transmuting over time into Athenian democracy, empowered a near totality of male citizens over a certain age. In theory, a more equal distribution of political power should have resulted in more equal distribution of ownership, and the creation of social peace. In reality, the Athenian Golden Age, which began about a century after Solon's death, was disfigured by war, despoliation and injustice.

The lesson remains: redistribution in pursuit of private enrichment may succeed, but usually redistribution fails if its object is to secure equality or justice. The propertied wield the most political power, and they vehemently oppose forced changes to existing property arrangements. Political reform intended to secure social welfare is more attainable, and may in time result in more equal distribution of ownership.

Possession and egalitarianism

Sparta, the enemy of Athens, supplies perhaps the most conspicuous example of an exception to the rule that a propertied class usually thwarts land redistribution undertaken for the public good. The Spartan counterpart of Solon is Lycurgus, a man said to be of royal blood, and credited by historians like Plutarch as the founder of the Spartan state. Lycurgus (born c 820 BC) lived nearly 200 years before Solon and is thought to have been a member of one of Sparta's two royal houses. As the Athenians turned to Solon to solve a social crisis, so the Spartans, in a time of social exigency, charged Lycurgus with reform of the political and economic systems of the city-state. Two hundred years before the Attic crisis, Spartan society had begun to break down because a small group of citizens accumulated and hoarded wealth, and dominated political decision-making.

Unlike Solon, Lycurgus brought revolution to his state (according to Plutarch, c 46–119 AD). He instituted social arrangements not wholly dissimilar from those of kibbutz socialism, although he did not disavow ownership. He decreed that private landholdings in Sparta and its Laconian hinterland be divided into equal indivisible portions allocated to male citizens, usually the heads of households. Sparta permitted women to own land, although the rule against subdivision was for centuries inviolable. Lycurgus required men to eat in dining halls in groups of about 15, and established the system of martial social organisation which facilitated Sparta's martial ascendancy in Greece, and its defeat of Athens in the Peloponnesian War 400 years later.

Unlike Solon – an aristocrat who did not wish to disturb the social assumptions of the Athenian aristocracy – Lycurgus sought moral reform. Amazingly, Spartans consented to the remaking of their society according to puritan principles: men are legal equals, men and women can be social equals, property is shared equally, a woman may inherit property, thrift is good, extravagance is bad, and the first duty of the citizen is to defend the state. Sparta, as constituted by the reforms of Lycurgus, is probably the most long-lived, authentically egalitarian state in the history of politics, albeit that its political system established a command-governed society. A council of kings and elders in effect directed an assembly of citizens who shouted their vote for resolutions.

For centuries after Lycurgus, Spartans continued to disdain commerce and make honour, constancy and valour their watchwords.

Then, in the century after the defeat of Athens, egalitarianism fell away. Constant warfare deprived the city of large numbers of its male population, and over time, the old pattern of wealth concentration reasserted itself. Speculators began illegally to buy the land of impoverished families and so to accumulate large landholdings. However, for nearly 500 years from the time of Lycurgus, Sparta offers the model of a society which refutes our presumption that a coalition of power and wealth must defeat attempts to create more parity in ownership.

Link between state and property system

The problem of possession is a problem of wealth concentration. Wealth concentration is more than majority ownership of wealth by small groups of people. It is also the creation of social settlements that favour or disfavour people. Social settlements are politically contested, and the winners of the contests make the constitutions and rules of a society. Invariably the allocation of advantage results in wealth concentration and the instrument of concentration is a property system.

We can observe this much in the reforms of Lycurgus and Solon. The former dispossessed the traditional controllers of property and political power. He created a new possessory system. From then, one Spartan family possessed land in only the same amount as any other family. In a society in which few possessed more than others, the urge to dominate dissipated, and the Spartans disposed of burdensome hierarchy, display, waste and many other things (including the barest acquaintance with literary cultivation).

Unlike Lycurgus, Solon had no wish to undo the pattern of social life. In Solon's lifetime, Athens was a society beginning to aggrandise itself, although its social precepts were rough and rude. It was not known for its literature or philosophy. It was divided between rich and poor, and the rich were unregenerate about maintaining the divide. Solon did little to reduce aristocratic power in the city-state. But he did prevent the rich from swallowing the estates of the poor, and started the body politic on the road to a kind of universal male suffrage. He did little to prevent the Athenian property system from entrenching the political advantage of the rich, including the aristocrats. The upper classes remained considerably in possession of the state, notionally and materially.

A lesson that we can learn from these two examples of political reform is that state and property system are inextricably connected, and the one, through the medium of politics, creates the other. Simplifying, we can say that to possess is to control. This message is at the heart of the writings of Karl Marx ([1848] 2002) who, far distant from Lycurgus or Solon, expressed a reality that is exemplified in the ancient politics of Sparta and Athens: dominant classes exploit weaker classes, and the advantage that they extract is measured in possession. Those who possess exclude those who do not.

3   Possession and exclusion

Control is expressed through property systems, which externalise power. To possess is to exclude. The property system of settled societies arises from the contest for sovereignty, and through the property system, people establish social and economic hierarchies which allocate more or less power to social groups.

Who, whom?

Thousands of years of social history testify to the immense social difficulty of reconciling the aims of people in society, of fashioning consent to government structure, laws, rules of behaviour, types of command, economic praxis, and so on. Reconciling aims and achieving a workable social consensus involves agreement about a source of authority and consent to the rules prescribed by authority. Modern democratic societies, usually the product of long political evolution and the related growth of a convention of reason, usually distribute authority and economic benefit more evenly than societies in which political control is exercised by a bloc or cabal. However, contest for political or social advantage in any society is unceasing.

Control is expressed through property systems, which externalise the disposition of assets – and the allocation of power. To examine property systems is to find answers to Vladimir Lenin's dyadic questions 'who, whom?' (1921).[1] The *who* possesses; the *whom* does not. Statistics reveal extreme wealth concentration in all settled societies. Distribution of political power is also concentrated. This is true because wealth concentration, which confers on the wealthy political influence, can nullify the possible benefit for many citizens of casting a vote. However a person without wealth votes, that person does not determine who in society is advantaged the most, and

DOI: 10.4324/9781003188766-3

who receives the most benefit. If voting much altered the distribution of benefit in society, wealth distribution in democratic societies would not be as unequal as it is.

A property system is inevitably exclusionary because it confers possession – which legally is the right to exclude trespassers – unequally. Property is the right of refusal. The right of refusal is the right to refuse others' access to (or possession of) the thing owned. Whoever disobeys a prohibition of access is what, in common law systems, is called a trespasser. If what is legally owned is owned because of the right of refusal, it follows that ownership or possession is exclusionary. If the property system is regarded as a sum of exclusions it can be seen as powerfully reinforcing both social advantage and disadvantage.

If I own a house you are excluded from ownership of that house: thus, to the extent that I own, you do not own, irrespective of the fact that you may yourself be a householder. From proprietary exclusion comes social inequality. The more you own, the greater your power to exclude. Ownership need not be exclusionary of course. An owner can declare a trespasser a licensee and adopt a permissive attitude to access. The more, however, that owners exercise their primary right of refusal or prohibition the more that the propertyless exist in a state of vassalage.

Process of exclusion

History involves constitutional reckoning. To live together productively we must together determine rules of society and reach agreement about the source of authority. The Crown is a source of authority, and is the more powerful because it does not reside in the person of a king or queen but instead is an abstraction apart from any person. Similarly 'we the people', identified in the constitutional text as the United States' source of authority, is a symbol commanding allegiance – allegiance granted by the public to something corporate, not *someone* or some *group*. Allegiance is given to the corporation 'the people', and then to the office of President insofar as the President is acknowledged as the people's primary representative.

The lesser and greater constitutions made throughout history determine social progress or retardation. *Who, whom* is decided wittingly or unwittingly by our compacts. The next great political innovation is anybody's guess. Constitutional growth conforms to a pattern, the *who, whom* pattern of contesting for and securing self-advantage. In other words, society is the product of a contest of competing sovereigns. The successful sovereign creates society's source of authority.

Command by a minority is in the nature of things political. Few would dispute the constitutional superiority of three great republics Athens, Rome and the antebellum United States when compared to contemporary political systems established elsewhere. Yet they functioned in effect by the fiat of a few belonging to a small class, that is, they did not express an articulated general will. All admitted slavery. Today, democracies apparently answer to the volition of a much more representative totality of voters, but the interrogative 'who, whom?' invites the same answer, when asked of our modern democracies, as it did when formulated by Lenin: a coterie of self-interest.

Sovereignty

Sovereignty results from contest, which is constitutional process, and one sovereignty substitutes for another, endlessly. However slow the process, we choose the society we want, which is why nothing is socially impossible. Governments could maintain citizens on permanent and bountiful doles, and invent true societies of leisure, if we and they wanted. But we do not know what we want and nothing preempts the slow movement towards some kind of social consensus. However, while constitutional arrangements are plastic, the constitutional or constitutive process, the working out of a source of authority, is objective.

When we compete over time for sovereignty, individually or as a group, we create and use property to sequester whatever advantage we have accrued. What is mine is mine and what is yours is yours – or perhaps mine. The more contested the source of authority in a society the more likely that distribution of resources or benefit is uneven. If authority is contested people fight more nakedly for advantage, invoking one or other particular representation of authority, and by refusing unity undermine the possibility of social progress. The property system in constitutionally unstable societies invariably creates a social supremacy of a minority, the minority with most power to enforce its will.

As it happens, even in more distributive societies – in which the population as a whole accepts the constitutional source – contest for sovereignty results in exclusionary property systems. But greater consensus about the source of the authority means more social unity, which is demonstrated in greater social willingness to co-operate for a common purpose. A good suzerainty – an authentic commonwealth – supplies a symbol that binds *ab initio*. A commonwealth permits the possibility of progress towards less unequal distribution. But wherever the source of authority is enforced, that is, assent is coerced, that source is not self-validated in the minds of citizens and the possibility of social progress is almost nil.

CASE STUDY – ROMAN REPUBLIC

Social conflict

The pattern of politics and social growth in Athens and Rome is in some aspects similar, although their political arrangements were markedly different. Both began as societies of tribes ruled by kings. In both, the deposing of kings and remaking of tribal structures resulted in aristocratic governance, and aristocrats continued to dominate politics after the definitive ending of Athenian democracy (322 BC) and the Roman republic (27 BC).

The political history of republican Rome is consumed by the struggle of 'people' against aristocracy, the former searching for equal representation and equality before the law. The social history of Athens is also characterised by a strong and unchanging polarity between rich and poor.

But the politics of Athens is unlike that of Rome. In the former, over time, direct democracy became a reality. Poorer citizens could speak and vote at a legislative assembly, but democracy did not obviously assist them to change their economic status. The Athenian proclivity for fighting other Greek cities, most disastrously Sparta, encouraged citizens to focus on outward threat: the war effort, especially during a successful phase, can transform domestic discontent into patriotic enthusiasm. During the period of Athenian democracy, lasting over 160 years, Athens sometimes resembled a military state, and it paid the price of too much militancy: it first became Macedonia's vassal, then Rome's.

Contrasting with the greater social equilibrium of democratic Athens, the whole of Roman republican history involved social struggle. Poorer Romans, comprising most of the citizen population, struggled against economic and political oppression. The struggle began as a fight between aristocracy and plebeians over legal rights, and became a long contest over entitlement between the landed rich and the landless others.

In Athens, Solon, appointed *archon* in 594 BC, enlarged the citizens' assembly, divided citizens into four property classes with different political entitlements and created a citizens' court. He cancelled debts and bonds, abolished citizen slavery, and refused to redistribute big estates. He thus partly enfranchised the citizen body, although he did not permit the lowest class of *thetes*, mostly poorer labourers, to vote. In Rome, after the exile of the last king, Lucius Tarquinius

Superbus (509 BC), a decades-long struggle between aristocrats and people produced a republic which ostensibly divided powers equally between an aristocratic senate and popular assembly, and distributed executive responsibility to various state officers, aristocratic and plebeian.

Roman aristocrats seemingly acknowledged the principle of parity when the Senate agreed to the institution of the office of tribunes (the people's magistrates), acknowledged the plebeian assembly's legislative power, and accepted the Canuleian law. The law, passed in 445 BC, allowed intermarriage of plebeian and patrician. However, the Senate's apparent openness to conciliation masked a fixed intention to preserve the primacy of wealth. For over 400 years, the republic wrestled with the social problems caused by concentration of wealth and power. Senators usually seemed unable to separate the wishes of the rich (many of whom were plebeian in origin) and the needs of the state.

Although at an early stage in its history republican Rome achieved theoretical equality between Senate and people, great Roman families controlled politics partly by exploiting the weakness of the popular voting system. Outside the Senate, Romans voted in three assemblies. Votes could only be collected from voters present at plebeian and tribal voting assemblies, and plebeian voters frequently could not or did not attend assemblies. The Senate, which controlled the machinery of government, capitalised on the popular assembly's legislative ineffectiveness to increase the stranglehold of the wealthy classes over Rome's economic and social affairs.

Contest of aristocrats and people

Aristocrats in both Athens and Rome dominated politics, as can be seen especially in Roman history. Aristocrats and the wealthy opposed with violence the four main attempts in republican history to make some change to distributive arrangements. In 486 BC, the Senate ordered the beheading of the consul Spurius Cassius, who proposed the first agrarian law to effect redistribution of public land. In 439 BC, the Master of the Horse, G. Servilius Ahala, murdered a wealthy plebeian, Spurius Maelius, after a patrician, L. Minucius Augurinus, accused Maelius of treason for arranging poor relief. (During famine, Maelius had bought a large consignment of wheat to provide food to the starving.)

In 392 BC, Marcus Manlius Capitolinus, a patrician hero of the Gallic siege of Rome (c 390 BC) and consul, sold part of his estate to relieve plebeian debtors threatened with bondage. The Senate declared that by his action, Capitolinus had tried to make himself king, a capital offence in Rome punished by hurling the condemned person from the Tarpeian Rock. In 384 BC, the Senate's executioners flung Capitolinus from the rock.

Finally, in 132 BC and 123 BC, the Gracchi brothers Tiberius and Gaius, plebeian nobles and tribunes of the people, sought, among other things, to revive the Licinian laws and redistribute largely appropriated public land. Both also proposed poor relief and Gaius advocated the unpopular measure of granting citizenship to the citizens of Italian states allied to Rome. Senate mobs murdered Tiberius and hunted Gaius to suicide.

In 88 BC, 35 years after the death of Gaius, Rome descended into a civil war between the *optimates*, who asserted the aristocratic claim to Roman primacy, and the *populares*, who stood for the rights of plebeians and the poor. Generals seeking power for themselves – Marius (*populare*), Sulla (*optimate*), Gnaeus Pompey (allied to Sulla), Julius Caesar (*populare*), Brutus (*optimate*), Marcus Antonius (*populare*) and Octavius (*populare*) – warred repeatedly during the next 60 years. Finally, Octavius – Augustus Caesar – declared himself Princeps Civitatus, the First Citizen and first emperor of Rome. Other than Sulla and Augustus, all of these men died violently or proximate to violence.

For Rome especially, failure to counteract the poison of extreme wealth concentration proved socially disastrous. Slaves worked the estates of wealthy landholders, and they grew ever-more plentiful. In the last century of the republic, slaves comprised perhaps a quarter or even one-third of the population of Rome itself. In the provinces slaves were fewer in number but in places might constitute more than one-fifth of the population.

A superabundant, ubiquitous slave population is evidence of an incapable society. Certainly, an argument could be made that by the end of the republic, and during the imperial period, Rome pursued war to replenish the supply of slaves, and perhaps depended for its existence on their labour. Slave labour suited principally the requirements of the rich, who thought nothing of displacing from work and home armies of provincial labourers, most non-citizens.

In the republic's last century, and afterwards, unemployment plagued the provinces and metropolis. Supplanted by slaves, many of the landless poor tramped to Rome, joining the city plebeians in idleness and corn dole subsistence. Roman civic endeavour languished and its philosophy and science advanced hardly at all. Even before the end of the republic, Roman politicians, representing wealth and class protection, cynically offered the populace *panem et circenses*, 'bread and circuses', a phrase coined by the satirical writer Juvenal (c 100–127 AD). They calculated that a stupefied population could not protest against whatever political manipulation suited their purposes at a particular time (Juvenal: 78).

Thus political failure engendered social failure. In Rome, wealth concentration corralled the majority of people in poverty and idleness, and deprived them of the possibility of meaningful life. In Athens, politics did not create a division of idle rich and idle poor but it did little to relieve poverty. The polity, directed by the rich, was more preoccupied with military struggle than social improvement. In both cities, too few owned too much. Athens and its Attic hinterland became a province of Rome and then Byzantium.

Republican Rome became imperial Rome, and eventually, in the 5th century, the western empire lapsed into political nullity. Yet many Roman social arrangements continued to exist. Many of the ancient estates, worked by slaves obedient to an absolute ruler, continued for centuries to function as they had before the fall of the empire. These estates became feudal estates, and the feudal aristocracy adopted the Roman mode of servile production.

The Roman senators bowed to the demands of the plebeians and admitted the principle of political equality between citizens. But voting requirements undermined the legislative power of the assemblies, and the Senate controlled the machinery of government. Frequently, the people's tribunes waived their extraordinary power to veto acts of the Senate because they, enjoying the prestige of office – and the Senate's flattery – identified their duty with the wishes of the wealthy.

In practice, the wealthy classes represented in the Senate gave up little, and politically emboldened, they placed no check on their accumulation of wealth from conquest or the appropriation of public land. The Senate's more unregenerate members ordered the murder of some of the plebeian representatives who demanded more equal distribution of power or benefit. In the end, the intransigence of the wealthy resulted in civil war and the destruction of the republic.

In its last century, the Roman republic was little more than a gangster state. The first triumvirate, the alliance of Julius Caesar, Marcus

Crassus and Gnaeus Pompey which began in 60 BC and ended in 53 BC, was the epitome of gangsterism. Each of senatorial family – Caesar a patrician, and Crassus and Pompey equestrians – these men manipulated Roman politics in order to receive governorships of the provinces of Gaul and Illyrium (Caesar), Hispania (Pompey) and Syria (Crassus). Crassus was the richest man in Roman history and Pompey wealthy from his conquests. Both were former consuls. Crassus subsidised Caesar's campaigns for political office, including for high priest in 63 BC and consul in 59 BC. Thereafter, Caesar enriched himself from plunder from the conquest of Gaul.

Between them, the trio helped to precipitate civil war, but intriguing for political control depended on money, and to usurp the state required a vast amount of money. Crassus, having bought himself a province, died in an ambush in the deserts of Parthia, trying to prove himself, aged 62, a conqueror. After his death, the alliance of Caesar and Pompey ended, civil war broke out again, and Caesar's armies vanquished those of Pompey. Led by Brutus, *optimates* of the Senate murdered Caesar on the pretext that he planned to make himself king, the deadliest of crimes against the state, and civil war broke out again.

Caesar's nephew Octavius emerged victorious from the war and established the rule of emperors. In the imperial period, the problems of wealth concentration and social inequality were no less pressing than they had been before. Imperial Rome lasted for about the same length of time as had republican Rome. The remedy for social immiseration remained bread and circuses, slaves continued to provide labour for most economic activities, and the rich, accumulating land and importing and exporting goods and produce, continued to grow richer. The senate remained as a supposedly consultative legislative body. In reality, it was obedient to the wishes of the emperor, the supreme executive of the empire.

The ancient histories of Athens, and especially Rome, tell us about the ultimate social cost of wealth concentration. A wealthy society must make a political decision to hoard or share surplus, which can be defined as distributable output, the meaning of which is also determined by political decision. A decision to hoard surplus is a decision to hoard power, and its opposite, a decision to distribute surplus, is usually made only when the wealthy agree to share political power.

Athens and Rome acted to avert class warfare by sharing power, with the result that Athens became a democratic state that gave male citizens an equal right to debate and pass decrees and laws. But neither polity prevented the rich from enforcing their will by the exercise of political privileges connected to wealth. In the case of Rome especially, manipulation of legislative rights and control of administrative functions allowed senators to dominate state decision-making. The rich chose not to be bound by constitutional rules, and the rules could be flouted by ruthless and self-interested people. Concentrated wealth and its concomitant in the ancient world, concentrated power, led finally to social breakdown.

Note

1 Lenin asked these questions at the All-Russian Congress of Political Education Departments on 17 October 1921.

4   Crypto-freedom and privacy

A property system confers privacy but also creates exclusion since property is owned – even if jointly – exclusively. The owner excludes the trespasser. The trespasser, potentially, is the whole world. Despotic dominion, in the words of Blackstone, means that within a property system people compete to possess things, and the exclusionary nature of ownership is expressed in ownership of the most by the few.

Crypto-freedom

Those who claim that liberal thought and liberal society have emancipated humanity from bondage make two mistakes. The first is to assume that a very short span of history during which many people have come to enjoy autonomy undreamt of by their ancestors predicts a future of increasing liberation. The second is to ignore that what imprisons people socially is not only one or another retrograde philosophy but the existence of an inevitable system[1] that exists regardless of philosophy: the property system. A property system can simultaneously liberate and imprison, in which case we encounter a paradox: crypto-freedom.

Perhaps the greatest freedom conferred by a property system is that of privacy. The word property derives from the Latin *proprius*, 'one's own', and if we own something, our exclusive enjoyment – or more accurately possession – of that thing creates privacy. Privacy enables us to know the dignity of selfhood away from the madding crowd. In small ways and large, ownership enables us to realise a central human aspiration: that of self-determination.

However, to paraphrase Marx's famous invocation of the spectre of communism haunting Europe, we are haunted by the spectre of crypto-freedom. To possess is to dispossess. To own is to exclude. One person's privacy may diminish another's privacy. Self-determination is covalent with separation: inevitably, my want is not your want and so our wants may divide us. The

DOI: 10.4324/9781003188766-4

crypto-freedom of property is that it allows possession to exclude possession. If A owns a thing, B cannot own that thing. If B owns nothing, B is destitute.

Of human bondage

Property systems through the ages have distributed power. We can say that a property system *is* power. All societies grow from constitutional settlement, and adapt and develop according to our constitutional settlements. What do we *agree*? The more we sincerely agree on the disposition of things or benefits in society the more likely we are, by our actions, to provide an egalitarian answer to the question *who, whom*? The less consensus the more likely that the answer to *who, whom* is anti-communitarian. The great social problem that the most famous earlier civilisations, Egyptian, Greek and Roman, could not resolve was how to distribute power in a way that did not inordinately benefit a small number of people while excluding a majority from benefit.

Their response was to create slave economies: they withheld legal rights from a large proportion of labour, which is to say that they practised non-reciprocal feudalism. A distinguishing feature of feudal or slave-dependent societies is social stasis. Very few members of such societies rise above their station meaning that social relations are petrified: generations of slaves or generations of peasants are servile to generations of uber-folk, the enfranchised who possess property and can self-determine. Servility represses innovation. In servile societies, warfare often becomes the principal means of survival and meaningful trade, commerce and culture are by degree stymied. Labour is forced rather than reciprocated.

CASE STUDY: FEUDALISM

After Roman jurisdiction broke down in western Europe after the 5th century, the Frankish Merovingian kings exercised political control over much of western Europe. In the 8th century, Charlemagne acceded to the Frankish crown and created the Carolingian or Holy Roman Empire from Frankish, Germanic and Lombard (Italian) territories. Following the empire's 9th-century collapse into chaos and war, a system of feudal tenure, responding to political instability and threat of violence, began to emerge in western Europe.

Landholders, small and larger, pledged themselves as vassals to martial protectors, exchanging title to their land for their lords' military protection. The lord became owner and the vassal became tenant of a fief, that is, alienated land in which the tenant holds an estate. A hierarchy of vassalage emerged which determined subordination of one class to another, beginning with peasant or serf and ending in service to the supreme lord, the king (who in turn owed allegiance to God). The practice of subinfeudation permitted grantees of fiefs, from the great lords to lesser nobility, to grant subordinate fiefs, the holders of which owed duties to their lord and king. Some lords, however, received fiefs unsubordinated to the fiefdom of any other title-holder by direct gift from the king. These nobles were tenants-in-chief, the peerage, who owed duties to the king alone.

In England after the Norman conquest, political and property systems co-identified the Crown as the source of constitutional authority. The Crown was, before the 13th century, legal innovator, interdicting, or trying to prevent, practices undermining its supremacy, such as franchising, subinfeudation, church land acquisition, alienation of estates and the use of trusts to escape liability for debts. The Crown, declared by the conqueror the source of authority for law, political action, title and conveyance, remains in England, and some other common law countries, title-holder-in-chief, authorising conveyance in fee simple, which, in theory, is a grant of lease. The legal system, instrumentally compelled to uphold constitutional settlement, is, in obeying that settlement, conservative and reactionary. It *conserves* the settlement, as it is constitutionally bound to do, and *reacts* to systemic challenge by doing whatever political consensus deems the constitutional settlement to require, including protecting the property system.

Under the manorial system that accompanied the growth of feudalism, the manorial lord, himself vassal to a greater lord, extracted rent from two classes of small tenants, or serfs: freemen, who were exempt from dues that indicated servility such as *merchet* (a payment due by the peasant to the lord for permission for his daughter to marry), and villeins, who tilled the lord's land as well as their own. Although they laboured gratuitously for a lord, villeins owed dues additional to rent. Cottagers owned a cottage dwelling and sufficient land for subsistence. Below them, slaves formed part of the lord's manor, and laboured for subsistence.

The freeman, who might be obliged to supply military service, paid rent to his lord and he and his household cultivated their acres for themselves. Serfs provided unremunerated labour to their lords for many days of the year. The serf paid other dues, including relief, heriot, tallage, toll and mortuary. The serf could not quit the lord's manor without permission, and for the privilege to leave must pay a fee. The lord in effect granted his tenants usufruct contingent on satisfying fiscal obligation, but a right of subsistence was not more than a necessary device to maintain the obedience of a servile population. It could not be said, as some commentaries argue, to constitute consideration provided by the lord to institute a contract of service.

The inferior titles of feudalism were designed always to benefit, and enrich, the lord.

The outcome of the struggle for sovereignty is property systems governed by constitutional settlements which may result in written constitutions. The settlement may be revised or overthrown but the same possessive urge causes settled societies to apportion entitlement to things. A property system is the composite of possessive intention expressed in the allocation in society of things material and abstract.

By appropriation we mean that people notionally, in language, annex and possess their external world. Most importantly (for our purposes) possessive language creates antithesis: if that thing is mine, it is not yours. If I own x, you do not. If you own y, I do not.

A property system reveals two things: who possesses the state, in its broadest meaning, and who does not. Who benefits most, who least. Possession and exclusion are consequentially related. If few possess, more are excluded. If more possess, fewer are excluded.

Possession and social separation

It becomes obvious why Rousseau lamented, in his *Discourse on Inequality*, the act of the hypothetical first person who enclosed a plot of land and 'took it into his head to say this is mine'. The act of possession, if Rousseau and others are to be believed, is one of alienation. Legally, more than one person can possess the same thing equally. In other words, more than one person can own the same property. But title is indivisible. Two people may possess and own the same property but what is owned is singular. The thing owned or possessed must be defined, and what is defined as the subject matter of ownership is not usually alterable. To own something is to possess the thing against the world.

Ownership is thus a radical social event. The English jurist Sir William Blackstone, in his *Commentaries of the Laws of England* published between

1765 and 1769, described the exclusionary character of property in words well-known to many lawyers of the English-speaking tradition:

> There is nothing which so generally strikes the imagination, and engages the affections of mankind, as the right of property; or that sole and despotic dominion which one man claims and exercises over the external things of the world, in total exclusion of the right of any other individual in the universe.
>
> ([1769] 2008)

What is striking about Blackstone's description of property is his emphasis upon its absolute and exclusionary character. Property confers on the owner 'despotic dominion' over external things 'in total exclusion' of any other person's right. Property is undivided sovereignty. Blackstone makes clear in the ensuing pages of his *Commentaries* that property, or at least sufficient property, is a source of power. Its power derives from the right to exclude. If you possess enough things exclusively, other people will want access to what you possess. They may want what you possess. Your power to deny access or refuse transfer of possession is the power to control others: if they want access to or possession of your property, they must do what you demand.

Note

1 The statement that a property system is retrograde is not a statement that property itself is retrograde.

5 Social consequences of ownership

The social consequences of ownership are profound. What is possessed becomes a legal object, which means that trespassers are excluded from the thing legally defined. The abolition of private property in collectivist systems does not resolve the problem of ownership or the natural desire to control external subject matter. A system of no-property is characterised by anomie. Ownership is connected to identity, which means that an agreed source of authority creates licitness in a property system, which in turns suggests the possibility of distributive agency.

Social consequences of ownership

Marx asserted (1848) that the French Revolution was, above all, a revolution of the bourgeoisie, which swept away feudalism and announced a new age of capital – and private property. Nothing is nearer to the hearts of the bourgeoisie, as characterised by Marx, than property. At the beginning of the revolution, the French National Assembly issued the *Declaration of the Rights of Man and of the Citizen* which asserted that 'the aim of all political association is the preservation of the natural and imprescriptible rights of man' including 'the right of property' (1789).

In the 20th century numerous international conventions, such as the 1948 United Nations' Universal Declaration of Human Rights and the 1953 European Convention on Human Rights, declared a human right to own or possess property (UDHR Article 17; ECHR Article 1). That they did so is hardly surprising. They in effect restated declared political rights that have in some way inspired most social struggle since the 18th century – the rights of man and the citizen declared during the American and French revolutions.

The social consequences of ownership are profound, as Rousseau and Blackstone pointed out. More than a half-century after the agents of Thermidor put an end to the Jacobin Club and the insurgent phase of the

DOI: 10.4324/9781003188766-5

French Revolution, Marx, a student of revolutionary France, promised the inevitability of the abolition of property. In the *Communist Manifesto*, Marx argued that property relations governed social relations. The more a person owned, the more power, in all the dimensions of power, that person exercised in society (Marx and Engels, 1848).

Marx's theory unleashed nearly a century of revolution, collectivism and political authoritarianism. The communist nations that subscribed to his doctrine usually abolished private property. Communism ended for interconnected reasons but a chief cause is that prohibition of ownership suppressed the human urge to freely make and multiply things, to engage in commerce, or to exercise the 'despotic dominion' of which Blackstone wrote in his Commentaries, and thus exclude the rights of 'any other person in the universe'.

Communism created in citizens what the French sociologist Emile Durkheim, writing in 1893, called 'anomie', a condition of social alienation engendered, in the case of many collectivist countries, by what could be called sham politics. Rejection of communism was a positive act of affirmation: by disavowing communism people showed that they wanted to enjoy the benefits of possession. Repudiation of communism revealed that suppression of individual choice made people unhappy. The strength of people's preference for free society illustrated the strength of what seems innate in humans: a desire to possess and own (Durkheim, 1893, especially Chapter 12).

Yet these desires are the source of strife, contention, hatred and willingness to engage in the darkest kinds of human behaviour: cruelty, fraud, murder, war, despoliation, theft. In the last 2,500 years, various writers have warned against the social dangers of possession and accumulation. Yet they do not explain much about the nature of possession. They agree that possession is potentially an evil. Rousseau, as we have seen, wrote of the enclosure of land by someone who said 'this is mine'. By that act of possession, the encloser, according to Rousseau, unleashed crime, misery and horror.

CASE STUDY – SPANISH AMERICAS

A more recent historical example of a great empire that could not resolve the problem of identity is that of Spain in the Americas. Perhaps the foremost political legacy of Spanish American history is constitutional void. In the 30 years following the enactment of Mexico's first constitution in 1824, the country changed government

48 times. In most Spanish American republics, politicians rewrote and replaced constitutions with a regularity that testified to the precariousness of politics and society.

Since independence, Ecuador has enacted 20 constitutions and Venezuela 17. El Salvador, Honduras and Nicaragua have each promulgated 14 constitutions, Costa Rica and Guatemala nine constitutions, Mexico seven and Argentina six. Colombia has had between six and ten constitutions (some constitutions applied to specific parts of the country) and Peru between nine and 18 (some are military statutes, some were short-lived and one early constitution pertained to a Peru–Bolivia confederation). Chile has had between seven and 11 constitutions (depending on how a constitution is characterised), most repealed before 1833.

Constitutions are political compacts intended to bind people. To a considerable extent the model of land settlement that prevailed in Central and South America after the Spanish conquest created a continuing crisis of identity, and later, constitutional uncertainty. Settlement in the Spanish Americas from the end of the 15th century reproduced a type of land organisation that emerged on the Spanish peninsular during the *Reconquista,* the reconquest over about six centuries of the Iberian territory annexed by the Moors.

The *Reconquista* began when the armies of the undefeated northern kingdoms embarked on a long liberation war, gradually moving southwards and ejecting the Moors. The possibility of receiving *encomienda* grants from the kings of Spain, that is, considerable gifts of land, became an inducement for noblemen and knights to take up arms, as well as reward for distinguished service. The recipients of these grants became quasi-feudal landowners, entitled to exact tribute from both the displaced Moors and peasants cultivating small landholdings within the *encomienda*. An *encomienda* grant signified both commendation of the *encomendero* and the necessity for him to honour the King's trust. The right to exact tribute implied the obligation to protect and care for those subject to his power.[1]

The Spanish carried the *encomienda* system across the Atlantic to the Americas. After the first Spanish settlement in Hispaniola in 1492, and particularly after the conquest of Mexico in 1521, the Spanish Crown granted certain settlers licences to *encomiendas*. A property system that channeled reward to a Spanish elite[2] survived for 300 years because of the Crown's prepotence as a symbol of authority.

When after 300 years the Crown departed, the source of authority vanished. The problem of constitutional void has plagued the countries of Spanish America since the date by which most of those countries had secured effective independence.[3]

As much as any factor which helps to explain retrogression in Latin America, the absence of an undeniable, unchallenged symbol of constitutional authority frustrated the liberation cause. Since a source of authority commanding popular allegiance could not be found, competing forces contested to fill the void. Since 1830, Latin American politics has usually shifted between left and right, between degrees of liberalism, illiberalism, collectivism and, latterly, neo-liberalism. Repeatedly, governments have failed because none is able to authentically declare itself endorsed or empowered by a constitutional source of legitimacy, one to which the population consents, as, for instance, the Spanish population consented to the basal authority of the Spanish crown, or the British population consented to the British crown as the source of legal right. In Latin America, legitimacy is absent because consent is a sham. The history of Spanish America shows us how property systems, inseparably linked to the evolution of societies, economies and cultures, are socially determining because they express consent or its absence. If consent is withdrawn, a property system breaks down. Social exclusion is one significant consequence.

Social inequality

The ordinary meaning of the word 'possession' is 'the state of having, owning or controlling something'. In the material world that humans inhabit, possession is a concept that explains ownership. Something is owned because it is possessed, and to possess the thing owned, thereby causing ownership to subsist, a person must measure what the thing is – that is, define the thing – and declare exclusive control of the thing, which means the power to exclude all others from entry on the thing or use of it.

The thing possessed is thus alienated for legal purposes: it becomes a legal object. By this process, all things material can be measured, alienated, called property and made subject to the control of owners: houses, cars, clothes, shoes, personal computers and so on. Things abstract that can be given material form can be turned into legal objects: a computer programme, for instance. In Rousseau's hypothesised state of nature, the absence of ownership precluded argument over things. Once humans created property they apportioned it unequally, allowing some to appropriate surplus while denying to others a share of surplus, or any property any all. Naturally, if some own on a large scale, and some own considerably, and some more than a little, and others own not much, and others own nothing at all, those who own less may feel unhappy. Unhappiness may turn to misery if exclusion from property reduces people to poverty and desperation.

Rousseau was the first thinker in the modern secular European world to call social inequality Europe's most important social problem. For centuries before him, writers, excepting a few thinkers like St Thomas Aquinas and Thomas More, paid little attention to the social effect of great wealth disparity. But long before Aquinas, writers of Christian apologetics, part of that group of expositors later known as Fathers of the Church, wrote on inequality. These men lived between the 2nd and 8th centuries in the Roman and post-Roman world of North Africa, Byzantium and Italy. They argued that possession of goods and wealth separates humans from nature, and from each other. Like Rousseau, they said that the creation of property and the desire to possess more and more things poisoned human relations and caused social misery.

Aquinas, author of *Summa Theologica* ([c 1265–1274] 1989), agreed with the patristic writers that property is a consequence of original sin. Unlike them, he said that although natural law does not support property, it does not forbid its creation. More, the author of *Utopia* (1516), argued that if property exists utopia (or to be accurate, a commonwealth) is impossible. Adam Smith (1776) wrote that:

> Wherever there is great property there is great inequality. For one very rich man there must be at least five hundred poor, and the affluence of the few supposes the indigence of the many.

Smith went on to say:

> Civil government, so far as it is instituted for the security of property, is in reality instituted for the defence of the rich against the poor, or of those who have some property against those who have none at all.
>
> (Bk V Ch 1 Pt II)

One of the Church Fathers, St John Chrysostom, said in a homily about the social effect of possessiveness:

> But as soon as soon as someone tries to appropriate a thing to himself by making it his private property, strife begins; it is as if nature

itself were aroused over the fact that, despite God's efforts to keep us together in peace and harmony by all possible means, we are intent on being torn asunder in our attempts to acquire private property and private possessions. Yes, nature is aroused by the very mentioning of the metallic words 'mine and thine'. From that moment the battle was joined and all vileness began. But wherever this 'mine and thine' is unknown, there exists no struggle or strife. From all this should follow the community of possessions is a more appropriate form of life than private property. And this community of all possessions is also more according to nature.

(Chrysostom, [386–398] 1950–1951: 169)

As Radin (1925: 207–28) pointed out, Roman lawyers from around the 1st century BC, and probably earlier, referred to possession as the chief characteristic of property. The word *possidere* came into English legal usage in the first half of 14th century. The law of property connaturalised concepts of possession, occupancy, ownership and control. It followed the precepts of Roman law, which from an early date recognised rights of possession and exclusion. When the Emperor Justinian codified the Roman law in the 6th century, he referred to possession as something more than ownership. Ownership permitted an owner to use the thing owned. Possession permitted the owner to use *and* modify the thing (Radin).

The civil law and later common law legal traditions adopted the Roman law concept of property as a thing that is possessed by its owner. When Rousseau referred to possession, he referred to the ordinary meaning of the word and also its legal meaning. We can possess something, meaning that thing is in our custody, without owning the thing. To own something we must have legal title to the thing, which usually – although not always – we obtain by paying the previous owner to transfer ownership. But the right of possession – of custody – is essential to ownership.

The problem of exclusion is directly linked to the problem of inequality. Although exclusion and inequality are different words with different meanings, as social phenomena they are closely connected. Social inequality occurs because of social exclusion. If some in society have more, and some less, the disparity tells us objectively that those who have less are excluded from more. Unequal distribution is a permanent social reality – which pertains also in collectivist societies – but the cause, nature and extent of exclusion are matters that properly demand analysis.

Notes

1 The relationship between *encomendero* and those paying tribute was quasi-feudal because unlike vassal relations pertaining elsewhere in Europe, it was more approximate to rent arrangements.
2 First Spanish-born then native-born of Spanish blood.
3 About 1830 when Simon Bolivar, the so-called 'liberator' of Spanish America, died.

6 Wealth concentration

People make possessive covenants about things and each other, and these covenants amount to a social consensus about what is right or not and the nature of authority. A source of authority exists insofar as society consents to the authority. Eventually, extreme social inequality leads to some or total withdrawal of consent. The abolition or reform of instruments such as trusts or instrumentalities such as intellectual property laws will reduce social inequality and provide means for the creation of societies of human flourishing.

The property system

A property system is not self-conscious. Like an economy, it is an unaware composite of human activities. Like an economy it can be studied and its workings disinterred. Human social activity is always determined by one or another compact, and people may formalise the intent of their compacts in a written constitution. From compact comes distribution. At every stage of social development power is exercised by someone or other. A formal constitution establishes power relations and distributes power. The process is organic. But each gambit for power and control is self-conscious and deliberate (Dworkin, 1977: 153).[1]

Power distribution is more than the distribution of property and ownership. But the one type of distribution simultaneously effects the other. The simplest way to disinter the property system is to examine the public record of ownership and entwined histories correlating the emergence of types and instruments of ownership with struggles for political, social and legal domination. In other words, to demonstrate the thesis that in the property system wealth concentrates, and exclusion is thus endemic, we need to provide instrumental evidence of concentration.

DOI: 10.4324/9781003188766-6

This is easy enough to do by analysing the growth of trust, corporate and intellectual property and land law, the historical instruments of concentration.

Trusts as instruments of wealth concentration

Trusts, creatures of the common law legal system, are, and have been for 800 years, concealment devices that create phantom ownership. The trustee, said to be the owner at law, is in reality the executor of a trust deed. In the executor's role, the trustee is unable to dispose of trust property except in accordance with the deed. In practice, the trustee is often not so much executor of the deed as a surrogate giving effect to the will of the true owner.

Who is the true owner? Frequently a person who wishes not to be identified as the owner of assets but who may wish to benefit from the disposition of assets. The trust enables such a phantom owner to exercise phantom (though also real) control over asset disposition. Trust assets of extraordinary magnitude may subsist as ownerless *seeming* orphans, that is *ownerless* assets that, within the legal meaning of possession, are disposed of by the trustee but not possessed by the trustee. The trustee, whom the textbooks declare is the owner of the assets, exercises possessory right only as the trust deed permits.

In tax havens trusts find both safe harbour and a natural home. Phantom ownership began in 13th century England when the Norman aristocracy, struggling for power against Plantagenet kings, invented the *fee tail* to avoid Crown impost or confiscation. Fee tail permitted by primogeniture perpetual accession to the trust estate. The first significant challenge to the legitimacy of trusts came during the reign of Henry VIII, when the king embarked on a broad-reaching fiscal campaign to enrich the Treasury for his purposes. In 1535 Henry secured passage of the *Statute of Uses* which converted some entailed estates to freehold. A freehold estate is owned and therefore taxable. Crucially, though, Henry did not dare to maximally challenge the upper-class sodality of phantom owners. Trusts could be converted but they could not be abolished and so trusts, in various forms, continued to offer opportunity for avoidance (as they later enabled investment).

The second challenge came when in the later 17th century the court in equity enunciated the rule against perpetuities,[2] which was designed to prevent perpetual survival of the trust estate. As developed, the rule against perpetuities reduced the utility of land trusts but reform did not touch the higher nobility who continue to observe the principle of primogeniture.

If we say *a priori* that phantom ownership is anti-social – because it is directed towards avoiding the tax authority while retaining control of the putatively taxable thing – we can see that trusts are powerful contrivances for accumulating, retaining and concealing wealth.

How much wealth is held by trusts is unknowable since so-called off-shore trusts located in tax havens are usually not required to submit meaningful financial reports in the relevant jurisdiction. Trusts located in ordinary jurisdictions file tax returns but are not required to disclose assets. Zucman (2017) has estimated that USD 8.7 trillion is held in offshore trusts but the real figure is not known.

Trusts permit a 'true' owner of assets to direct asset disposition through the terms of a trust deed administered by compliant trustees. If the true owner is a phantom, his or her assets remain hidden from scrutiny. As a repository for undisclosed assets, trusts may be (from the true owner's perspective) more useful than companies, and in the jargon of tax professionals, more 'tax efficient'. The 800-year history of trust law reveals one particularly salient social fact: if politically influential people, who are probably members of the same social classes, wish for the maintenance of a particular privilege, the state will comply with their wish. For this reason many trusts live mostly unexamined lives, by their nature inimical to government, functioning as repositories of ownerless capital, out of sight and usually out of legal reach of authority.

Companies as instruments of wealth concentration

While trusts are the creation of a class rejecting authority, the modern public and proprietary company originates from collaboration between State and traders seeking to get rich abroad. Modern corporate law starts at the beginning of the 17th century, when both the English and Dutch states chartered respective East India Companies to establish trade markets in India and beyond. The French Crown chartered the French East India Company for the same purpose in 1664. In 1711, the British Crown chartered the South Sea Company to trade in Spanish America (its principal proposed activity was to transport slaves) but predominantly the South Sea Company functioned as a large-scale creditor to government.

These gargantuan public-private enterprises, designed to create markets and hedge risk, gave way in the 19th century to purely public (and private) companies that in Britain pressed against the trade monopoly of the East India Company. In 1825, Parliament repealed the Royal Exchange and London Assurance Corporation Act of 1720 (the 'Bubble Act' 6 Geo 1, c. 18) that required potential public stock companies to be, like the East India and South Sea companies, chartered or established by legislation.[3] Then in

1844, Parliament passed an Act (the Joint Stock Companies Act 1844 7 & 8 Vict. c. 110) providing for corporate registration and allowing for registered companies to be viewed as entities distinct from their members. As distinct entities, they could (in the name of certain office-holders) sue or be sued. Companies now possessed individual corporate identity or personality.

Company legislation passed by the British Parliament in 1855, 1856 (superseding an 1855 Act) and 1862[4] respectively extended to the shareholders of registered companies the protection of limited liability, which is the principle that a shareholder's liability for company debts is limited to the value of the shareholding. Banks were permitted by 1858 legislation to incorporate as limited liability companies, and the 1862 legislation extended the benefit of limited liability to 20 insurance companies.

Connectedly, in 1858, Britain declared its Raj in India, absorbing the administrative functions of the East India Company. This event signified the beginning of London-incorporated stock companies undertaking huge colonial investment, their members protected by limited liability. Within a few years of the passage of the 1862 Companies Act, the world's commercial landscape was transformed by the global effusion of British, European and US capital.

It would be difficult to overestimate the effect on the growth of world capital markets of statutory and judicial acceptance of the doctrines of individual corporate personality and limited liability.[5] Most would agree that the capital investment and technological innovation that has shaped the modern world would not have occurred if corporations were not empowered to contract personally and limit investment risk.

So far as inequality is concerned, even cursory analysis of financial reports and other literature tells us that limited public companies have greatly enlarged and concentrated wealth since the 19th century. Today the capitalisation of the New York Stock Exchange is about USD 21 trillion, the NASDAQ[6] USD 17 trillion, the two primary Chinese exchanges an aggregate of USD 11 trillion, the Japan Exchange Group USD 6 trillion, the Euronet Exchange USD 4.6 trillion and the London Stock Exchange USD 3.5 trillion.[7]

The combined value of share capital raised in a handful of the world's leading industrial countries is thus about USD 66 trillion or USD 66,000 billion. Most stock is owned by financial corporations, especially banks. Individuals and families own about 3% of stocks. The 30 biggest controlling shareholders[8] of these listed companies owned or controlled over 50% of the assets of the companies. The compilers of these statistics described them as evidence of the 'financialisation of ownership' and noted that, '[t]oday the world is dominated by corporations that follow the logic of finance capital – the logic of money' (Peetz and Murray, 2017).

Intellectual property as an instrument of wealth concentration

Confluent with the evolution of trust and corporations law, itself connected to the extraordinary growth of economic output in the 19th and 20th centuries, intellectual property law changed the way that people thought about ownership and property. The concept of property in things abstract radically enlarged the compass of proprietary exclusion. The concept, formally developed in the 19th and 20th centuries – although the origins of copyright law can be traced back several centuries – dematerialises property.

In other words, under the auspices of intellectual property law, legislators came to recognise that property can subsist in that which, although it must be realisable in material form, does not itself have material form. Thus copyright in literary, artistic, musical and dramatic works, and the material fixations of these works, as well as patents in novel ideas, and designs and trademarks, which visually identify companies engaged in commercial activity.

Intellectual property law is a creature of international treaties. Thus it is pervasive throughout the world. It is also, from a regulatory perspective, the source of the wealth of the intellectual property industries. The wealth of software, communications, internet, film, music and many other industries is dependent on the suasion and enforceability of copyright law. Similarly the suasion of patent law is critical to the continuation of a great range of technological industries, including the pharmaceutical industries. International protection of designs and trademarks enables companies to propagate a corporate identity for the purpose of trade.

Each of these industries, to the extent that they enforce intellectual property rights (IPR), is exclusionary. The social consequence of exclusion is connected to the problem of access. IPR creates monopoly for certain time periods, which means that for those periods monopoly pricing and access prohibition precludes consumers and others from gaining utility, instruction, diversion and pleasure from subject matter protected by IPR. One social consequence of preclusion is constraint in the exchange of ideas. Another is constraint in, and degradation of, public discourse. Preclusion, effected by exercise of the primary right of ownership, that is the right to exclude, has a delimiting effect on the transfer of knowledge (from developed to less developed countries, for instance) and freedom of expression. IPR constitutes a vital element of national and global property systems, and the world trade system.

Exclusion generates wealth. The extraordinary wealth of people and companies connected to the entertainment, communications or software industries is a product of copyright monopoly, and equally the patent monopoly confers what sometimes appears to be inordinate wealth on technological innovators, individual and corporate. For present purposes the important fact is that IPR functions to concentrate wealth and consequentially exclude from access to information large numbers of people throughout the world. The wealth of intellectual property industries, because many members of those industries are listed companies, is significantly discernible in stock market capitalisations.

Property systems

The history of commercial law, especially in the past two centuries, illustrates the thesis that the growth of a property system is coincident with the elaboration of rules of ownership that benefit a social minority. The House of Lords gave judgment in the momentous *Salomon* case,[9] about 20 years after Britain acquired (or began to acquire) its second empire, larger than any other in history. Before and after *Salomon,* joint stock companies embarked on decades of enrichment in colonies that themselves offered markets but also provisioned the British domestic market. After the dissolution of European empires, more or less by the beginning of the 1960s, corporations continued to trade in world markets, their viability revealed in balance sheets and share registers.

Estimations of wealth distinguish between financial assets (non-tangible wealth) and non-financial assets. Accurately surveying asset-holdings is difficult, since wealth-holders are not obliged to (or choose not to) declare all assets. However, a United Nations-sponsored survey in the first decade of the 21st century provided a rigorously compiled survey of world wealth distribution (Davies et al., 2006 et seq.). Two of the lead authors of that report have continued to make principal contributions to Credit Suisse's annual Global Wealth Report (2012–2020), which systematically appraises world wealth distribution.

Analysing these reports, we can say that wealth between nations and the individuals within nations is extremely unequally distributed. Another way of stating the proposition is to say that Gini wealth coefficients show chronic wealth concentration in every world jurisdiction. Richer countries do not invariably concentrate less but they are better able to maintain social stability (and we could say social happiness) because they are richer. The cake is divided in a similar way but it is larger, usually much larger.

Most of the wealth concentration discussed concerns corporations. But wealth is also concentrated in domestic residential markets. Rates of home ownership vary between jurisdictions but consistently the operation of monetary and fiscal policy in most developed world jurisdictions has reinforced the trend towards inequality. In many instances the central banking authority has become a guarantor (or would-be guarantor) against large corporate failure, increasing liquidity and debt which inflates asset prices – which in turn increases wealth concentration, deflating the purchasing power of lessees and prospective residential property purchasers.

The future

The main types of economy practised by societies throughout history are slave, feudal and contract. The modern contract economy arose as the feudal estate transformed into a freehold estate. We have seen how the human drive to own has seen the creation of property systems that, by their nature, cause social inequality, apportioning to a small minority the most social benefit. Governments' response to the economic contraction that followed the onset of the Covid-19 virus epidemic is debt spending and monetary expansion.

In August 2007, immediately before the world economic crisis, the United States' Federal Reserve Bank's balance sheet was USD 870 billion. By November 2008 it had more than doubled.[10] By late 2014, after four phases of quantitative easing (or government buying debt), it had quadrupled to about USD 4.5 trillion. At the time of writing it had grown by a factor of seven, to over USD 7.4 trillion.[11] In the first period of monetary growth, the European Central Bank added USD 2.3 trillion to its balance sheet[12] while the Bank of Japan and Bank of England added nearly USD 2 trillion to their balance sheets: in 2020 the United Kingdom's quantitative easing portfolio totalled around 30% of nominal UK GDP, while that of the Bank of Japan represented 104% of GDP.[13] This money in turn increased asset values maintaining the value of bank loans and enlarging stock prices.

Yet wealth in itself is not an object of government redistributive policy. Wealth's continuing immunity from taxation is to some extent explained in Thomas Piketty's (2014) formula $r > g$, which asserts that the net rate of return to capital (r) exceeds the growth rate of output (g). This is so because capitalists arrange for accumulation to exceed investment, and a greater rate of accumulation means concentration of benefit that might otherwise be distributed. The reluctance to consider wealth as a target of taxation, as opposed to income, means that no obvious means exists to reduce inequality.

The extraordinary value of stock market capitalisation, which dwarfs government capitalisation, which in turn points to the extraordinary aggregate value of other private assets, tangible and intangible, tells us that enough wealth and income exists to substantively assist in some resolution of the world's economic and social problems. However, because of the way that property systems function or are permitted to function, wealth redistribution is stymied.

Some redistribution could take place without substantively disturbing the interlocking relationship of government and capital, which, given the human linguistic-mental-social proclivity for property, appears to be a necessary one. Policy of this kind would mean that government ceased to be second-resort indemnifier of capital and instead became a capital distributor. Let us imagine a future in which one-tenth of the capital value of all public companies, let us say about USD 7 trillion in total, is made available in liquidity to fund social projects. Let us say that government begins to operate in a way somewhat akin to those in the propertyless ideal societies proposed by Plato (c 375 BC) and Thomas More (1516). That is, they are disinterested and act for the common good uninfluenced by special pleading. What kind of society might government then usher into existence?

It might involve a vast increase in, and cultivation of, public space, investment in technology that reduces the need for employment, creation of a leisure economy to occupy a leisured population, the establishment of driverless transport systems that collect and deliver people from and to their doorsteps, and at-cost access to information, pharmaceuticals and other public goods. Additionally, let us imagine that trusts, other than trusts for charitable purposes or the maintenance of those without legal capacity, are abolished. No doubt several trillion dollars worth of capital would be made available for taxation. Or if abolition is judged too radical, imagine the requirement that trusts publish their capital holdings and tax is levied on those holdings.

Covenants, consensus and consent

The chief lesson emerging from the preceding analysis is that people make possessive covenants about things and each other and these covenants amount to a social consensus about what is right or not and the nature of authority. When people repudiate covenants society's fabric is stretched a little and if they (we) withdraw our consent to more socially significant covenants, the fabric of society tears, sometimes irreparably. Once consent is withdrawn a society can collapse quickly, as is the case when some major political coups occur, such as the Russian (or Bolshevik) revolution. Societal collapse does not necessarily mean ruin in a conventional sense. The creation by Bolsheviks of a communist state did not mean the end of Russia but rather a new dispensation with one source of authority substituted for another and a new legal regime instituted.

Consent – which involves submission to (though not necessarily approval of) authority, or the source of authority, or the sovereign's right to exercise authority – is authority, that is, it is indispensable to the existence and working of authority. All things in society depend on consent. The mystery of why things happen in society is not a mystery: things happen because A initiates and B consents in some way sufficient, for whatever reason, to allow A to do whatever A proposes.

We can imagine what might happen if populations at large withdrew consent to economic policy. Central and commercial banks would probably cease to function since monetary policy is predicated on the presumption that economic output must increase and asset values must be protected (with the result that asset bubbles, which increase social inequality, become unending). Withdrawal of consent would mean conventional bankruptcy for banks and other institutions although society would reform and start anew. As great revolutions demonstrate, consent can suddenly vanish and things considered immutable such as banking and security systems can dissolve. Yet society continues and consent is given anew to things new and different.

One factor above all seems to be bring one society to end and allow another to form in its place: inequality. When inequality becomes too gross, and the dereliction of the powerful insupportable, the old ways end as consent is withdrawn. In the words of WB Yeats, 'Things fall apart; the centre cannot hold'. Society, then, is mutable and imagining a better way to allocate resources than pertains in the present is meaningful if we imagine that our centre is beginning to fail. Let us imagine a hypothetical society that is worth discussing because it is theoretically feasible. Vast, almost unimaginable, wealth exists in the world and is owned by a tiny part of the world's population.

Were a portion of that wealth, let alone the whole (and not forgetting that wealth is a chimera of sorts existing only because we consent to its existence), made available to create public goods, then many of the world's problems could be solved. The objection invariably made to redistributive proposals is that redistribution kills incentive and therefore fails because productive resources are unutilised. This may be, but the proposition has not been proven. Let us imagine therefore a way to effective redistribution. The foremost method would be to abolish trusts except for trusts directed solely towards public good or welfare or maintenance of minors or the infirm. The abolition of trusts would inevitably disgorge hidden money and of course could not be achieved without reform of international tax law, but such an action would not result in confiscation. It would instead flood the economic system with money. We can then imagine positive government action utilising increased tax revenues.

Notes

1 Ronald Dworkin's theory of rights as 'trumps' could be argued to be a theory
 of the paramount value ascribed by legal systems to private interest (even if the
 private interest is the sovereign in a totalitarian society). In western legal systems, enforceable private rights, typically proprietary, 'trump' considerations of
 majority benefit: 'rights are best understood as trumps over some background
 justification for political decisions that states a goal for the community as a
 whole.'
2 Duke of Norfolk's Case, 3 Ch. Cas. 1, 22 Eng. Rep. 931 (1682).
3 The Act forbade the formation of joint stock companies except by royal charter.
 The East India Company and South Sea Company were chartered, and in the
 early 18th century owned about 85% of capital on the London Stock Exchange.
 In theory the Act precluded any other competitors (unless they could be chartered) from trade as stock companies.
4 The Limited Liability Act 1855 (18 & 19 Vict. c. 133), Joint Stock Companies Act
 1856 (19 & 20 Vict. c. 47) and the Companies Act 1862 (25 & 26 Vict. c. 89).
5 At common law, the case of *Salomon v Salomon & Co. Ltd.* [1897] AC 22 upheld
 the doctrine of limited liability. Salomon incorporated a company limited by
 20,006 shares of which he owned 20,000 (and family members the remainder).
 Upon insolvency he arranged payment, in priority to unsecured creditors, of
 debentures issued by the company to him. The Court of Appeal criticised his
 conduct but the House of Lords considered that Salomon's fiduciary duty was
 different in specie from the obligation owed by the company to repay debt.
 Salomon, despite his principal role in its affairs, was *not* his company.
6 National Association of Securities Dealers Automated Quotations exchange.
7 https://www.tradinghours.com/markets-by-capitalization.
8 From a pool of more than 2,100 shareholders who held a controlling share of
 listed companies analysed.
9 *Supra.*
10 https://www.federalreserve.gov/monetarypolicy/bst_recenttrends.htm.
11 https://www.federalreserve.gov/monetarypolicy/bst_recenttrends.htm.
12 https://www.ecb.europa.eu/pub/annual/balance/html/ecb.eurosystembalanc
 esheet2019~fed8c5244a.en.html.
13 https://www.bankofengland.co.uk/-/media/boe/files/paper/2020/the-central-ba
 nk-balance-sheet-as-a-policy-tool-past-present-and-future.pdf.

Part II
Inequality and distribution

7 Paratrophic action

Paratrophic action is social behaviour that arranges compulsory transfer of benefit from one actor to another. Paratrophic action leads to social inequality. Controllers of politics and economies create conditions for the concentration of power and wealth, the wealth compact, and by so doing act paratrophically. Paratrophic action can be ameliorated and to some extent overcome by government or public action.

Wealth exteriorises control

Objectively, control is manifested in the design of property systems to transfer benefit to controlling groups.

Power and wealth converge to establish the control of the powerful and wealthy over the economic and social choices available to the majority of people in society. They create affiliation, and affiliation creates common purpose in any epoch. That purpose is *paratrophic*. The word paratrophic in its strict meaning refers to the act of an organism obtaining nourishment from living organic material. The word could be said to be a synonym for *parasitic* though we use it in a looser sense that differentiates paratrophic and parasitic actions. Paratrophic action can be ascribed a secondary non-biological meaning, one that refers to the compulsory transfer of benefit from one agent or actor to another. Paratrophic transfer, in this sense, is not parasitic because the paratrophic actor, while receiving transfer of benefit from the subordinate actor, provides a reciprocal benefit, albeit much smaller.

Controllers of politics and economies create conditions for the concentration of power and wealth, the wealth compact, and by so doing act paratrophically. If undisturbed by opposition or constraints of morality or principle, paratrophic action is ultimately consummated in the creation of societies dependent on slave labour. If morality forbids slavery, paratrophic

DOI: 10.4324/9781003188766-7

actors establish servile modes of production, be they called feudal or free market.

The free market is preferable to feudalism to the extent that it is free. This is to say that a market of any sort is constituted by contracts, and that market is only free to the extent that the contracts are voluntary and not procured by oppression or abuse of bargaining power. Given this explanation of a free market, it is obvious that even in modern advanced economies, regulated by the monitors of anti-competitive behaviour, the paratrophic tendency can flourish in governments' willingness to conciliate capital at the expense of labour and to make policy opposed by a plurality of citizens.

The societies of Athens, Rome and Latin America were paratrophic in economic organisation. Their property systems were considerably impaired by political failure that stemmed from failure to establish an agreed source of constitutional authority. The result: extreme concentration of wealth and political power, and acute social exclusion. Examination of the property systems of most countries, throughout history, reveals a similar pattern of concentration and exclusion, resulting in gross social inequality.

The paratrophic impulse, especially in advanced countries, is constrained by various factors: the existence of institutional antagonism – if it exists – towards collusive or anti-social behaviour, the relative efficacy of the democratic process, and the efficacy, if it exists, of property systems in distributing economic benefit. Yet so long as the compact of wealth exists in any country, paratrophic actors will continue to subvert distributive process. A paratrophic arrangement is one that transfers benefit from entity A to entity B on terms prescribed by B. Because it involves exchange, the arrangement is not parasitic. Entity B returns a benefit to entity A, but the preponderance of benefit accrues to B.

Against paratrophic action

Paratrophic action, however, is not irresistible. Since 1945, policy in developed countries has divided between affirmative response to John Maynard Keynes's (1936) primary theoretical insight, which is that government is the agent that must cure demand deficit by debt or fiscal spending, and the monetarist premise that government's most important role is to control the money supply and thus inflation. Keynes believed in the ameliorative power of government agency. His most well-known opponents, von Mises (1949), Hayek (1944 and 1960) and Friedman (1960 and 1962), by contrast, fetishised individual freedom as a consummate social object, the realisation of which depends on the operation of markets unconstrained by government misuse of its regulatory power. According to Friedman et al., the correct role of government is to cure market failure, control the money supply, and adjudicate market and other disputes.

Many people living in richer countries argue that the relative economic success of those countries and the consequent size of national income is reason to ignore concerns about wealth concentration. Gross output is sufficient, they argue, to ensure that enough is available for everyone. No one starves, and few die of preventable disease. Some inequality is a necessary consequence of variable contributions to output. A person who contributes more is entitled to more reward. By permitting unequal reward, society advances in material welfare and creates surplus that can be distributed for the benefit of all. If taxation shrinks reward unduly, contributors (sometimes called 'wealth creators') will lose incentive to contribute.

According to the argument, extraordinary wealth concentration in the United States, to take one example, is tolerable so long as 'wealth creators' are liberated, by tax reduction and deregulation, to create more wealth. More wealth means more income, which means more money available to governments for social spending. This argument, though easily caricatured, is correct in one particular. Rich countries *do* create sufficient income to support distribution of meaningful benefit to each member of the population.

In theory, if, as growth economists argue, output continues to increase sufficiently, disproportionate benefit to one population group does not preclude other groups from receiving sufficient benefit to report material satisfaction. Paratrophic action can be curtailed. Output expansion guarantees sufficient income to support social provision. From a distributive perspective, the growth argument fails because it is contradicted by the history of resource allocation. Distribution does not occur autonomously. It is directed, arranged and governed by humans affiliated with groups and institutions. Social history (as discussed in the case studies in this book) tells an unremitting story of groups paratrophically appropriating benefit and not sharing it. Unless the government intervenes positively to regulate the pattern of distribution, private individuals and groups will, abetted by government, appropriate a disproportionate share of benefit.

After 1980, governments, while not resiling from social spending, seemed to internalise the principle that government is an interlocutor between markets and voters. The argument between Keynesianism and other schools of economic analysis is a dispute about the role of social intermediation, which is a dispute about political control. Keynesianism assumes that government is a fiduciary while its opponents consider government a corporate agent, albeit one without much fiduciary responsibility. A government that accepts its fiduciary purpose fulfils, or seeks to fulfil, social objects. A government that functions as a corporate agent, such as the government of a tax haven, forsakes much commitment to social spending.

Social inequality: the sum of exclusions

If a property system is viewed as the sum of its exclusions, wealth lies in the right of owners to exclude others from access or possession. Property by its nature excludes. Expressed differently, those who possess or own wealth also possess the power to exclude from the benefit of their wealth those who possess less or not at all. Ownership *is* exclusion. To own a thing, a person must be able to control that thing, and to control the thing that person must be able to exclude another person, a trespasser, from controlling or possessing the thing. If the sum of proprietary exclusions is social inequality, it follows that if the ambit of ownership reduces, so too does the ambit of exclusion.

Lammers et al. (2008, 2012) have explained that when people feel powerful or entitled they also start to feel invulnerable and morally unconstrained. While the experience of ownership does not obviously predict feelings of power or invulnerability, if we believe that an object 'is mine', and 'not yours', we are likely to resist strongly government initiatives to separate us from what is 'mine' or 'ours', or tax us for owning an object that we *feel* to be part of us.

The strength of owner self-identification provides a reason for government to direct distributive efforts to what is most easily redistributed, namely personal or corporate income. The human tendency is to decide that gross maldistribution of income or assets is unfair. People reason axiomatically and fairness is an axiom to which they subscribe deontologically. That is, innately and automatically, people judge the fairness or unfairness of an action. Fairness demands (all things being equal) that people should partake of available resources equally. If nine-tenths of a population must divide one-third of total available resources, that majority (to say nothing of individual sub-groups within the majority) suffers material deficit compared to the one-tenth of the population to which is allocated two-thirds of available resources. Axiomatically, we say that such disparity in allocation is unfair.

Fairness and altruism are concepts that people *feel* as norms that ought to guide social behaviour. Depending on ethical education or the ethics of a particular society, people learn to uphold or disparage these norms. In other words, people natively recognise the moral value of fairness and then learn to avow or disavow fairness as a moral principle. People who criticise conspicuous distributive disparities do so not only because these disparities are judged to be unfair. Critics also recognise that they are socially detrimental. People sense intuitively that manifest inequality is wrong because it is likely to be the product of unfairness, and they recognise that too much unfairness destroys the possibility of social good.

Wealth distribution in a jurisdiction, or technically the distribution of net assets (tangible and non-tangible), reveals the disposition of power in society. Contemporary wealth surveys enable us to quantify disparity in a way that is not possible when analysing historical social inequality. Societal balance sheets, consisting of corporate and household records, including stockmarket capitalisation, shares of corporate ownership, records of asset holdings such as houses, accumulated land values, and the record of beneficial holdings, provide a measure that is more powerful than that of national income distribution in answering the question of who, whom? – *who* owns, *whom* does not.

Measuring inequality

While surveys of social inequality conventionally focus on income distribution, wealth distribution more accurately reveals the nature of inequality in society. Wealth, or what is owned (tangible and intangible assets), is more disparate in nature and hidden than income, which is disclosed in tax records. Because income is liquid and is redistributed through the agency of taxation, a record of income distribution can only partially show the dimension of social inequality. United Nations surveys (1990–2020) of national income inequality using the Gini coefficient (range 0–1, 0 meaning nil inequality and 1 that one person owns everything) reveal that the range of income inequality between countries lies approximately between 0.23 and 0.60. Most wealthy countries report a Gini of between 0.23 and 0.44 because these countries heavily redistribute national income by spending on social services.

By contrast, the counterpart mean Gini for wealth holdings ranges from about 0.55 to 0.90. The leading rapporteurs of worldwide wealth inequality, Davies and Shorrocks et al. (2006, 2008 and 2011),[1] have outlined the unyielding character of ownership: 'The global wealth Gini is ... 0.892. This roughly corresponds to the Gini value that would be recorded in a 10-person population if one person had $1000 and the remaining 9 people each had $1' (2006: 25). Separately, Shorrocks and Davies reported that,

> Our latest estimates for 2000[2] suggest a Gini value of 90.4 per cent [for worldwide wealth inequality], and a figure of 84.8 per cent for the share of the global top 10 per cent, close to the 85.1 per cent reported in Davies et al. (2011).

(2018: 3)

Unless by expropriation or divestiture, wealth is not redistributable, a fact which highlights both the intractability and extremity of its concentration in all countries. An unnoticed fact is that wealth concentration in the United States and other developed countries may be as high or higher than in many poorer countries. The mean wealth Gini of Denmark, Switzerland and the United States is about 0.80, a coefficient approximate to the wealth Ginis of some of the poorest African countries.

According to Shorrocks et al. (2018), in the period 2000–2015 the top 1% of wealth holders in a country typically owned 25%–40% of all wealth, and the top 10% accounted for 55%–75% of wealth. At the end of 2019, millionaires around the world – 1% of the adult population – owned 43.4% of global net worth. 54% of adults, with wealth below USD 10,000, owned less than 2% of global wealth (Global Wealth Report, 2020).[3] Data collected from a number of sources shows that wealth disparities between-countries and in-countries is acute. Other surveys of human development and happiness also show acute differences between countries. According to reports sponsored by the United Nations, wealthy countries that invest more heavily in health and educational services and report higher levels of institutional probity and trust rank the most highly for human 'development' and 'happiness' (Human Development Reports, 1990–2020 at http://hdr.undp.org/; Happiness Reports, 2012–2020 at https://worldhappiness.report/archive/).

The degree of wealth concentration is high, however, in *all* countries. Even during the Covid-19 virus pandemic, household wealth did not noticeably contract despite economic contraction. According to Shorrocks et al., 'asset prices – both financial and non-financial – either remained fairly stable or returned close to pre-pandemic levels by mid-year 2020 in most countries' (2018: 31).

Statistics demonstrate the thesis that property systems accrete power and control to small population groups. Wealth concentration throughout the world is acute and seemingly not prone to much variation. The human possessive urge, expressed in societal relations, appears to ensure that income and particularly wealth holdings are concentrated and disparity places societal control in the hands of a few.

Reconstruction

After the end of the Second World War, the United States led and financed a reconstruction program in western Europe and Japan that partly aimed to achieve more equal distribution of resources for the public good. The motives for postwar reconstruction were not overtly distributive: the United States wished foremost to transform the political systems of West Germany and Japan into stable and ethically compatible polities, and thereby generate economic conditions that would allow countries aligned with the United States to trade relatively freely. Altruism influenced the plan of reconstruction but the critical fact is that American subventions enabled western Europe and Japan to create both economic prosperity *and* a politics governed, as it had not been before, by distributive considerations.

After about 1948, many richer countries accepted social spending as a government obligation, and created so-called welfare states. These developments were not the direct consequences of the reconstruction program, but reconstruction and social spending shared a common ethos, one of public benefit. Not coincidentally, in western Europe and the United States, the postwar period till about 1980, which witnessed the establishment of varieties of welfare state and especially social spending on health and education, accompanied an efflorescence of expressive and consumer cultures, the leisure economy, technological innovation and social optimism.

Income redistribution effected by allocation of a large proportion of tax revenue to social welfare programs forms the fiscal background to social transformation in western Europe and the United States in the three decades after the Second World War. Policy debate about economic policy has fundamental consequences for society, but economic policy has had little positive effect on wealth distribution, and, except in the three decades postwar, declining influence on income distribution.

It has, outside the postwar era, done little to remedy the problem of unequal distribution and social inequality. To some extent economists and others have tried to redress this shortfall by devising measures of human development (judged by reference to indicia of longevity, health and income) and happiness (judged by objective/subjective criteria, namely GDP per capita, social support, healthy life expectancy, freedom, generosity and the absence of corruption). For all the cognisance of policymakers about the social effect of property systems, those systems might as well function far below the surface, like tectonic plates, which now and then shift, causing reverberations that destroy the elaborate social constructions of those who seek in the terrestrial world to control society.

The history of the world can be called the history of privatisation, or the growth of ownership. It follows that if ownership is possession and control, its opposite, namely what the Romans called res publica, the public domain, is also the domain of non-possession and non-control. In the public domain wealth inequality is no longer a predominant fact of social life. The lesson is simple: to reduce social inequality, reduce ownership. Enable the public domain to flourish.

Ownership is reducible in a number of ways, by confiscation, private gift, public purchase and taxation of wealth. The last of these methods is most commonly advised by the proponents of measures to reduce social inequality (Piketty, 2014). A wealth tax can be imposed on types of consumption, landholdings, inheritance and the transfer of capital. Of these measures, the least tried, and probably most intellectually popular, is the single tax on land, most famously advocated by Henry George (1879). Georgist economics posits that the imposition of the most tax on land that offers the most amenity for private and commercial purposes will create the machinery for a just and sufficient distribution of ownership. George remarked on the 'utter absurdity of private property in land!' (1885) but he did not advocate abolition of ownership, rather the abolition of economic rent. In theory, a single tax on land encourages the owner to vacate the property or put it to the most productive use, creating taxable revenue. The tax raised can then be used for community purposes.

Wealth tax is actually always income tax since assets are not physically redistributable, though they may be transformable. However reduction of ownership is effected, to reduce ownership is to reduce control, which is to say that what is private becomes public or unpossessed and what is public remains public.

More popular forms of wealth tax include taxation of inheritance or capital gains or luxury (conspicuous) consumption. What matters, though, if one goal of public policy is to reduce social inequality, is that the public domain is cultivated. Taxation is the sovereign path to cultivation of the public domain. But taxation is not the only way to reduce distributive inequality.

CASE STUDY – SINGAPORE

Singapore is known as an exemplar of a modern services economy, simultaneously a manufacturer and international distributor of goods and a provider of financial and other services. What is less known about Singapore is that the State owns about 90% of housing stock and 80% of citizens reside in State housing (Haila, 2016: 42). Also less known is that the governing People's Action Party (PAP), the party of government since Singapore's inception as an independent State in 1965, was founded in 1955 as a socialist party and only withdrew from the Socialist International in 1976 (Tan, 2020).

In 1955, Singapore was a British colony moving towards self-government (1959) and reception in the Federation of Malay States (1963). Singapore remained a member of Malaysia for two years until its separation from the federation in 1965. The People's Action Party espoused socialist principles as the means to conciliate labour and respond effectively to the problem of widespread poverty. In 1965, it had purged itself of Communist-affiliated members, and begun the task of creating a viable State by a program of poverty alleviation and economic growth (Tan, 2020).

By the end of its first five-year development plan in 1965, Singapore's Housing Development Board had constructed 1,031 apartments (Tan, 2020: 155). The PAP facilitated mass home ownership by purchasing land for the development of apartments on a large scale, and encouragement of home-purchasing through provision of access to the Central Provident Fund, Singapore's compulsory saving scheme for income-earners. In 1964, the government inaugurated a 'Home Ownership for the People' scheme. In 1967, the Land Acquisition Act gave the government power to acquire land for the purpose of housing construction and by 2010 the government had become owner of 90% of land in Singapore. Singaporeans could lease small or large apartments for 99 years or shorter terms (minimum 30 years), in effect becoming lifetime tenants who could dispose of their leasehold interests and purchase new leasehold as they wished (Tan, 2020: 156; Haila, 2016: 99).

Through so-called government-linked companies, which invest monies from the Central Provident Fund, the Singapore government holds a substantial minority share of the capitalisation of the Singapore stock market. Singapore owns a large proportion of eight real estate investment trust companies which in turn invest 54% of the total of monies invested in Singapore real estate. As of 2020, the overseas net property portfolio of the Temasek corporation, which invests Central Provident Fund monies in Singapore and overseas, is valued at approximately USD 350 billion (https://www.temasek. com.sg/en/our-financials/portfolio-performance). If the United States had accumulated proportionately a sovereign wealth fund equivalent to that of Singapore, its 2017 value would be more than USD 12 trillion.[4]

Eighty per cent of housing stock in Singapore is public housing and 90% of that stock is occupied by long-term leaseholders who are, in effect, owners of their apartments. The government has accumulated a huge property fund invested in domestic and mainly foreign property markets. In short, the State is not only lessor of the very large majority of housing stock, it is also a chief investor in stock and realty markets in Singapore and abroad. Its profits are public funds available for public investment purposes. Widespread home ownership (or its simulacrum) helped to engender a conformist society but one in which in one particular, that of housing, partly resolved the question that plagues most other countries, that of unequal home ownership. The result of mass ownership is a society that is partly Platonic, in the sense that government and legislature form an elite group that makes social rules, and partly Georgist, in the sense that the problem of concentrated ownership of land is resolved by State acquisition (which is not the prescription of Henry George).

Historical political and economic conditions in Singapore are largely different from those in countries in which unequal home ownership causes political and economic problems. At the beginning of the PAP's life a large proportion of the population consisted of Chinese immigrants who were not British subjects and a large proportion did not own the dwellings in which they lived. The PAP inherited the common law system but not a tenure system that radically vested in the sovereign and assigns (the aristocracy) control over land in the jurisdiction. The government could effect what governments in most other jurisdictions cannot: the progressive alienation of land for public purpose.

Even so, Singapore's success in creating near-universal public housing, while encouraging the growth of a market economy, testifies to the efficacy of government action to distribute ownership – in the form of housing (and property investment) – evenly throughout society. Sequestration of land, provision of building stock, compulsory saving, access to savings, and flexibility in disposal or purchase of property assets created a peaceful society of homeowners.

Notes

1 Anthony Shorrocks, James Davies and Rodrigo Lluberas update annual surveys on wealth inequality in the Global Suisse *Wealth Report*, https://www.credit-suisse.com/about-us/en/reports-research/global-wealth-report.html.
2 The basal year for the first report of worldwide wealth inequality. Subsequent reports by the same authors and others update figures collected from household surveys for 2000.
3 Shorrocks et al. reported in the 2020 Global Suisse *Wealth Report* (at 3) that, 'The level of world wealth inequality is exceptionally high'.
4 Article Matt Breunig. 9 March 2018. 'How capitalist is Singapore really?' https://www/peoplespolicyproject.org/2018/03/09/how-capitalist-is-singapore-really/.

8   Proposals

Possession and exclusion cause social inequality. In history, societies are shaped more by paratrophic action than public action. However, humans are capable of sharing as well as possessing. The private domain articulates or defines itself. The public domain, however, is ill-defined. Public and private can co-exist for the benefit of people but what is public should be defined as a domain that is protected as the public domain. A way to define and protect the public domain is to institute a Public Domain Authority funded by government and public donation, one which defines the boundaries and contents of the domain and advocates for the domain. The Public Domain Authority would be independent of government, functioning, for legal purposes in a way similar to that of statutory authorities such as federal reserves. By defining, enlarging and protecting the public domain an agency can assist society to achieve the object of human flourishing.

Purpose

This book identifies two truths about human behaviour: we possess, and because we possess, we exclude. Possession and exclusion cause distributional inequality, and associated social problems. As long as people wish to possess, society will be unequal.

Because our language insists on possession, we are trapped by a compulsion to annex everything around us. If we annex mentally, we soon enough annex physically – to the exclusion of others. Our natures are also disposed to sharing. A compulsion to annex and an impulse to share: we expend our energy in the never-ending mental cycle of trying to reconcile two seeming unreconcilables.

Possession and sharing are not, to borrow from *Henry V*, 'two yoke-devils sworn to either's purpose'. But we are capable of both possessing and sharing. You can simultaneously possess and share a house, though the acts of possessing and sharing are opposites. The greatest gift of possession

DOI: 10.4324/9781003188766-8

is privacy but in the realm of non-possession, privacy ceases to be a social object: now we share a public domain, from which no one is excluded.

In the public domain, none may exclude another from possession, since none possesses. In the private domain, you may exclude anyone from what you possess. Possession is proof against interference and a guarantee of safety. By contrast, if we possess nothing, we may be at the mercy of those who wish to harm or control us. In a domain of no-possession are we in a state of nature? Life in the state of nature, according to Thomas Hobbes ([1651] 2017), is nasty and short. The public domain is unlike Hobbes's state of nature. It is contingent, not primordial. That is, its healthy function depends on recognition by the sovereign authority. To flourish, it must be recognised and protected as a realm of non-ownership in which distributive competition does not exist. If nothing is owned, and anti-social or criminal behaviour is punished, it might be asked how exclusion is possible. Exclusion occurs in many ways. This book has examined the principal social instrument of exclusion, property. We exclude instrumentally by ownership. We do not, of course, need to possess things to exclude others. We make exclusionary social rules, and we apply those rules to ostracise others, to persecute, to kill on occasion, and to banish. Ownership, however, is our chief means of social separation and the law of trespass enforces the separation. If ownership ceases, so does trespass. In the public domain, the law continues to govern behaviour but the law of trespass vanishes.

So, substantively, does privacy. If no person can possess some portion of the public domain, others cannot trespass on that portion. The greatest penalty of forbidding ownership is the loss of absolute legal protection against the intrusion of others. No one may enter your house without your permission. But in a public park, you cannot forbid the unwelcome stranger from sitting next to you under a shady tree. The public domain would be intolerable to us as humans if we were without recourse to ownership. Then we would live in the worst dystopia that totalitarianism could impose – or in a state of nature. But existing parallel to, or interweaved with, a private domain, the public domain offers the opposite of dystopia, and a partial cure for the dystopia created by the pervasive ownership of a relative few. This book is not written as an exegesis about ownership and exclusion. The other chapters, by explaining the cause and effect of distributional inequality, invite this final chapter, which offers as a solution to the crises created by concentrated ownership a modality of non-ownership.

The public domain is both conceptual and physical, and to survive it must be protected by law. It is nothing more or less than that which is not owned. Nothing survives without protection. The world's history is a history of privatisation. That which is not owned becomes owned, and it becomes owned by force of law. The law protects what is private. If it does not, the private ceases to be private. A solution to the social problems arising from encroaching – and engulfing – privatisation and attendant ownership concentration is not necessarily to reduce what is private, although in theory ownership reduction ought to reduce social inequality, but to protect what is public.

A truism of property law is that what cannot be defined cannot be protected. Thus the first necessity of protecting the public domain is to identify and thereby define it. Once defined, the domain becomes the subject of legal protection. Once protected, it cannot be privatised. The public domain may consist of a rainforest or marine park protected against private appropriation, or anything purportedly owned by government (but in truth held in trust for a country's people), or the resources of nature, or the artefacts of national heritage. It may consist also of a notional repository of ideas, exchange, language, discourse and so on.

This chapter proposes three things, from which certain other things follow.

The first is that government and public join to map, like cartographers, the boundaries of the public domain, physical and notional, and its contents, physical and notional.

The second is that the legislature pass laws to protect the public domain, as defined.

The third is that government establish either an agency, or agencies, of the public domain, the purpose of which is to protect, uphold and advance the domain. Preferably, government could establish an *independent* public authority vested with the power to protect, uphold and advance the public domain, irrespective of government wish.

The remainder of the chapter is concerned with explaining each of these three proposals.

Map the public domain

The purpose of mapping the public domain is to protect what is public from encroachment, appropriation, privatisation; in short, extinction. Throughout history, the growth of civility, manners, cultivation, impartiality, fellow feeling, and openness to inquiry and speculation is associated with public exchange and public reception of the fruits of individual inquiry and expression. The concept of a public domain is akin to the concept of eudaimonia[1] espoused during the Athenian Golden Age. Eudaimonia is private and public. It is private because it is a moral state attained by the individual who deduces from human behaviour a teleology of right and wrong and chooses right. It is public because private virtue is expressed in public participation.

The same comment can be made about the *res publica*, the Roman concept of things in common, which gives us our word 'republic'. For the Romans, the republic was the Commonwealth, the expression of common good, indivisible from the state constituted by citizens acting not for self but for each other. History contradicted the Romans' assumption that they shared common purpose, but the truth remains that, through history, people have believed that in the public realm our better natures flourish, and we, emboldened by the principle of mutuality, shrug off the irksome claims of self. We shun the deadly poison of exclusion.

An argument about private and public that asserts contradistinction between the two correctly draws to our attention that one is not the other, but otherwise tends to divert us from a more significant point. Humans have, since some forgotten period of our species' attendance on the planet, compiled mental inventories and formal registries of what is ours, or what belongs to us, to the exclusion of others. Things owned are private. My house is mine, not yours. But we also share, and wish to share. Perhaps not our houses, but many things and activities, and possibilities. Our wish to possess and our wish to share may cause in us conflict but they may also operate in harmony. While owners have a bad habit of trying to consume what is public, we are mistaken if we assume that the history of privatisation, which is more or less history itself, predicts that the private must inevitably annex the public.

Anarchists such as Pierre-Joseph Proudhon (1840), Peter Kropotkin (1892), and more recently Nicholas Walter (1969), espouse an optimistic view of human nature which posits that humans can, and will choose to, co-exist cooperatively.[2] How the private disposes itself, and what happens to the public, depends upon individual and political choice. But history tells us that the public is like a child or an innocent: it must be protected against predation. If not protected, predators will certainly consume it. If it is protected, the possibility of human flourishing, of corporate human flourishing, invites and beckons us to enforce the separation between one realm, that of possession, ownership and private transactions, and the other realm of non-possession, non-ownership and cooperation.

The proposal is simple. Define the public domain. The private defines itself. Anything owned must be defined if the law is to confer possession, and the appellation 'property' attached to the thing owned. Whatever is private before the law is defined and notified, recorded. We can be in no doubt about what is owned, not least because if we doubt that something is owned, its owner is likely soon enough to appear to assert title. The same cannot be said of what is public.

Things public are not owned. Some things may be described as public property controlled or owned by the government but so-called public or state ownership is trusteeship. A government, state or any representative of a social plurality can only possess in trust for the plurality, usually an abstraction called 'the people'. However, these public assets 'owned' by government are usually identified in the same way that things private are identified, and as meticulously cared for and governed as things private.

Not always. Because government does not really own assets, it sometimes loses sight of them, or forgets their value, or why they are important. Thus the lazy decision to sell to a property developer disused buildings next to a river, and change the zoning of the property sold to permit residential construction. Or the decision to sell water rights to a company that destroys the aquatic ecosystem by diverting too much water to agricultural purchasers.

In these, and many other instances, assets are defined but they are not owned and conserved with an owner's solicitude. They are too easily lost to the public. In many other instances what is public is not known.

Who is the owner of that pastoral land on which farmers have encroached? What is the status of council houses if councils decide they do not wish to pay for their upkeep, or perhaps that budget problems could be fixed by demolishing the houses and selling the land, or selling properties in situ? What if the crown decides to convert bountiful crown land into freehold and sell to more developers? Or some authority decides to sell public parks? The public realm is not much protected, and still less known. How many orphan things, like orphan works, copyright works unclaimed by their owners, inhabit the public domain? How easily does the orphan's careless guardian cast it off? Take any public instrumentality uninformed about the inventory of things entrusted to its control. It is unlikely to resist if someone wants to acquire for a song this field or that copyright or that rundown public park, or such and such disused utility, or a languishing patent.

The instrumentality is then a negligent trustee, not a diligent owner. In this case, it probably finds difficulty explaining whence assets came and for what purpose. The instrumentality may sell the uncared-for stock for the price offered. Against this prospect is the prospect of protecting the public domain by charting its perimeter and depth with the exactitude of a cartographer. Define the domain and its contents. In each jurisdiction, conduct an audit, take an inventory. Create an entire map. Show, throughout the district, the municipality, the town, the city, the surrounding country, all public areas and their designation.

Then the inventory. What things are public assets, and who or what controls them? List all things known that are controlled by public authority or are orphans, unowned or uncontrolled by anyone or anything. Invite the public, that is the citizenry, to assist in the compilation of the inventory. What is in the public domain? Anything not owned. Things not owned includes public assets, the things controlled by state or government on behalf of the population. Objectors will instantly proclaim that many public assets, or things said to belong to the state, cannot be in the public domain because they are not available to the public and in most instances the controller of the asset positively prohibits access – the military for example prohibits public access to most of its assets.

The state also declares rules of confidentiality and secrecy to foreclose public access to a great deal of information that the state treats as its property. Laws declaring the state controller or custodian of assets – everything the state purportedly owns, controls and keeps private – may be exclusionary, and on occasion necessary, but they cannot deny the truth that the state is trustee for the people and cannot own anything. Thus public assets and public information treated as state assets and state information are the public estate, even as the public is separated from its estate. They are at the least the inheritance of the public domain even as the state forbids access.

No less important than the physical public domain, and not more difficult to define, is the abstract public domain. Most things intangible are describable and often embodied in the material form of books, recordings and so on. Their contents are also the public domain's inheritance. We can argue that notionally much public information, of manifold variety, subsists in, and enters, the public domain even as the state declares it secret or unavailable to the public. The secrets of governments, disclosed by whistleblowers, enter the domain, beyond retrieval by the pursuing state. Works out of copyright, lapsed patents, research without proprietary claim, types of information released for public consumption, information the legal status of which is contested: this and other material enters and forms part of the public domain. The domain physical and abstract is definable and vast. But its parts are vulnerable to appropriation. Things public can be privatised for private use or profit. Public and private do not detest each other. They are like husband and wife living separate lives in the same house.

Protecting the public domain

It follows that that which you identify and define for the purpose of protecting against its annexation is protected by law. Public authority cannot easily post guards to prevent agricultural or pharmaceutical companies from patenting the DNA of plants for profit. But the authority can make DNA extraction for profit illegal. First, of course, it must define the legal status of plants. Can their genetic code belong to someone? If so, whom? Will their uses be limited in certain ways? Or is flora and fauna part of the common estate, and thus the public domain? In the abstract, total ownership in any jurisdiction is the accrued property or assets in that jurisdiction at any time of survey, and is usually a cumulative total; that is, it increases over time.

A political event like the imposition of communism in a country may ostensibly reduce property holdings to near zero, especially if the political event is accompanied by a declaration of the abolition of property. However, as this book has pointed out, property abolition does not (despite legal declaration) extinguish ownership. Ownership as a condition exists everywhere, regardless of what laws say. Property is the legally enforceable right to exclude. Ownership is the condition of owning, that is, of possessing, and it also a condition of control.

Thus in a declared propertyless state, while no one owns property, some people exercise the power of control, a power usually conferred by state fiat. These people are crypto-owners. This book argues that to the extent that total property holdings reduce, distributive inequality reduces, because fewer people possess the means to exclude others. But as long as some people possess property, they can exercise inordinate social control because ownership creates control of others. For this reason, a domain of non-ownership must be proof against the claims of owners outside the domain. The domain must be established as an independent commonwealth exempt from control by owners of any description.

That which is unprotected by law is the object of predation, or, less dramatically, sequestration, enclosure and appropriation. The tragedy of the commons, so called,[3] is as much a tragedy of coming plunder as heedless overuse leading to indigence. If we uphold the public domain, if we wish for it, if we value things in common, and the act of sharing, and have no wish for nature and living creatures to be reduced by more and more appropriations, then we must protect what is in common. Present laws are not sufficient because they are partial and usually do not interlink. We need to map, and know the whole, and protect as public all things defined within the boundaries of the map.

Agency or authority

For those who see antithesis between the results of state and private agency, state activity is a signifier for waste, inefficiency, misallocation and sometimes corruption and turpitude. However, this depiction of the state-in-action, which is often a proxy remonstrance about the wickedness of authoritarian states, betrays ignorance of evidence, in the past 75 years, of the remarkable efficacy, for the common good, of state action.

The first consistent evidence of the state acting conjointly as a powerful and beneficial actor begins in the mobilisation of allied forces, and allied industry, to win the Second World War. Thereafter, it is obvious in the postwar reconstruction, designed and considerably funded by the United States, and the concomitant creation in a number of countries of a redistributive fiscal system, a system which provided funds also for an unprecedented commitment of assistance to poor countries.

It is not too much to say that some countries, such as the United Kingdom and United States, achieved for a considerable number of their citizens societies of at least partial human flourishing. To decry the value and potency of state action is to ignore the social achievements of certain states in the three decades after the end of the war. The truth of state efficacy in times of common purpose, when social need is great, and the public willing to embrace concepts of common good and common necessity, is undeniable. A concept of common good and common necessity such as that proposed in these pages calls for state action, and effective state action.

Once a public domain is mapped, and legislation passed to recognise its existence, boundaries and contents, more is needed. That 'more' is an entity: an administrator that is more than administrator, that is also an advocate and imaginer. Such a body might be a government department, but preferably it would be like a federal reserve charged with responsibility for monetary policy independent of government. Such as body, charged with responsibility for the health and welfare of the public domain, fulfilling the role of a preceptor for common good, directing itself towards the role of encouraging human thriving, could to some extent reverse the great ill this book has identified: the social exclusion created by the fact of ownership.

By acting in two capacities, one as administrator and the other as advocate, an independent statutory authority, which might be called a Public Domain Authority, could function as registrar of all things identified as part of the domain, and otherwise advocate for the cause of the domain, which is the cause of non-ownership, the antipode of the movement in favour of possession and privatisation. In short, the PDA could advocate for the public, as needs be, against the private, interjecting itself, as needs be, into substantive political debate and public controversy, sometimes in concert with government, and other times in contradiction of government.

It would become a distinct political caucus representing the domain, and by association, the public interest and the public. Such a statutory authority is unprecedented. The work of advocacy implies substantive research capability, which in turn alerts us to the most socially transformative aspect of a Public Domain Authority. If its purpose is to protect and advance an actuality we can call non-ownership, and propose policy that will enlarge society beneficially by hypothesising – and helping to realise – a reality of human flourishing, its ambit of policy consideration must be broad and enlightening.

The starting principle is that while the public domain co-exists with ownership and profit the domain itself admits neither profit nor ownership and exists distinct from both. The public domain is not a domain of equality. It is, rather, a domain in which inequality does not exist. It should not be thought that an enlarging public domain de-privatises that which is owned. On the contrary, the boundary between things owned and not owned should only alter to the extent that owners voluntarily, and without trace of coercion, surrender property. A great deal of domain enlargement potentially occurs because the mapping of the public domain discloses that things thought to be private, or disused and neglected, are what can be called state assets or unsecured by an obvious legal title.

Above all, the creation of a Public Domain Authority would permit social calculation seemingly beyond the capability of today's inheritors of the post-Second World War socio-political settlement. At present no government policymakers, or indeed academic theorists, can conceive of redemptive reform that is universally acceptable. The postwar settlement can be called redemptive reform. Its greatest intellectual contributor, John Maynard Keynes (1936), having spent his adult life grappling with the consequences of the destruction of the European social order, perhaps felt directed by circumstance to apply his intellect to the task of devising reform that was redemptive, as it had to be, and also workable.

A Public Domain Authority can offer something curative, because it would be emancipated from the social prejudices and stultifying ideologies which constitute the intellectual dead-end to which the settlement that Keynes helped to create has, despite good intentions, led. As a third force in politics (assuming its independent establishment), aligned neither to government nor private interest, a Public Domain Authority can perform practical and intellectual functions that contribute to voluntary redistribution and establishing policy directed towards social realisation of flourishing or eudaimonia.

Its purpose is to separate public from private, and uphold the public, which does not mean disavowal of things private. But an authority dedicated to what is public, and the public interest, offers the way to establish an alternative conception of social organisation that can exercise a direct effect on private action. A Public Domain Authority cannot participate in markets, or profit-making activities, but it can identify policy that could overthrow the panoply of supposed market practices that concentrate profit, wealth and benefit – practices including collusion, selective free trade, money politics, laws permitting monopoly and proto-monopoly, especially intellectual property laws, global acceptance of tax havens and trusts, and so on.

Human flourishing could be achieved if a Public Domain Authority explained how many things owned could be made free for all without damaging markets or undermining productive incentive.

Some examples explain how a Public Domain Authority could function and act as a policy advocate.

Reducing the scope of ownership

In one period of history, the thirty years that followed the end of the Second World War, a few polities, chiefly those of the United States and the United Kingdom, and a few European countries, most notably West Germany, entertained the idea not that the total of ownership or property should decrease, but that the benefits of both should be distributed widely in the population. To make social provision for the whole population and create for the population more access to societal and economic benefit, they relied on the instrument of taxation. Tax can be imposed on different items. To name a few:

- Income
- Inheritance
- Wealth (assets of all description)
- Unimproved land (wealth but taxed discretely)
- Luxury consumption
- Consumption generally.

History suggests that in the absence of special circumstances – such as the destruction of wealth and social hierarchies that occurred in Europe in the first half of the 20th century – and broad political consensus arising from those special circumstances, polities will not embrace a redistributive tax program that does what such a program must do in order to be effective – diffuse rather than conciliate wealth.

That is to say, tax policy will focus on income redistribution that supports social provision but does nothing to change the distribution of ownership. A polity supportive of tax to alter ownership distribution would tax inheritance, land, equities and luxury consumption. However, polities are not in favour of taxing the wealthy till the pips squeak. This does not mean that a Public Domain Authority should abstain from analysing tax policy to explain how tax might be applied to enlarge the scope of non-ownership in society.

A particular example of tax that may help to reduce ownership concentration, thereby reducing the exclusionary effect of property distribution, is land tax. As discussed, land tax is often cited by followers of the journalist and economist Henry George, the 19th century's bestselling advocate for distributive justice, as the means to create a machinery of sufficient (not equal) distribution. George considered land the source both of value and economic control. Tax land commensurate with its market value – signalled by actual or potential rents – and, according to George, the incentive to accumulate or speculate withers. Tax nothing else. Soon enough an unforced redistribution takes place and enough land is available for all.

Some countries tax unimproved land but usually as one of many taxes. The equitable unforced redistribution envisaged by George has not come to pass. But tax policy remains, and probably will for all time, a fruitful subject for discussion, revealing society's willingness or otherwise to contemplate significant reduction in – or redistribution of – things owned.

Voluntary redistribution

The long tradition of charity and opportunity shops selling donated clothes and domestic goods at prices affordable to those of few means provides a clue as to how a Public Domain Authority of sufficient resources could function to facilitate redistribution of things owned, but on a grand scale. Assume a Public Domain Authority with the resources of a large government agency: it could perform an extraordinary redistributive service by establishing an online facility to connect donors of money, property or services to prospective donees listed under categories of need; the service need not be confined to a single national jurisdiction, that is, it could connect domestic donors to potential foreign beneficiaries of provision. Such redistribution could only be properly effected if, once a thing is donated for a specific purpose, the donor surrenders control over the thing, since continued control over the disposition of the thing continues the donor's ownership.

Public housing stock

The example of Singapore, to which (as discussed) pertains particular social, economic and historical circumstances, supplies an example of beneficial government action to create mass ownership (actually leasehold) of what is probably the largest asset acquisition of an ordinary citizen in an ordinary lifetime: residential property or the family home. Although the social and political circumstances of Singapore are unusual, and its population relatively small, it shows that relatively even distribution of residential property does not preclude free-market dynamism. In Singapore's case, social spending is, compared to that in other advanced countries, relatively low. For this reason, many elderly citizens work in menial jobs to supplement or provide a pension. But most people possess a home that is substantially paid for. The model of government adopting as one of its key policy initiatives the acquisition of land and provision of dwellings, as well as flexible access to superannuation for the purpose of home acquisition, is one that applies to relatively few jurisdictions. It is also one that provides a route to distributed ownership and thus less social inequality.

Energy

Debate about climate change and energy policy is mired in unproductive conflict. A Public Domain Authority could provide independent and authoritative advice on the constructive ways to facilitate an adoption of renewable energy generation that is consistent with exploration of the idea of costlessness (see next section). Harnessing renewable energy is one important way to de-pollute the public domain. Similarly, a Public Domain Authority could analyse and advocate ways to reduce waste, including plastic waste, in the public domain.

Costless society

A dream of many social thinkers has been to enable the creation of a costless society, a utopia realised by society consenting to use technology for non-proprietary purposes. In a costless society, law is no longer the servant of the wealthy. Technology has reduced price to unit price. In this dream, the three hundred-year-old contest between capital and labour is resolved by merger. The social contract between capital and labour, if compacts between contestants can be called a social contract, dissolves, because compact is no longer needed. As technology is distributed, law ceases to act as the instrument of the wealthy.

Technology, as its future function is envisaged, reduces transaction costs, social and economic, almost to nullity. Labour is no longer oppressed by the owners of technology. Technology is no longer an oppressor because ownership of technology is no longer concentrated. It is distributed and technology comes to exist, ownerless, for public benefit.

Technology relieves humanity, or that portion of humanity fortunate enough to live in technology-directed societies, of substantial need to labour. Competition ceases to govern economic activity because distributed technology makes access to an enlarged public domain equally accessible to all. Society surrenders to technology, acknowledging that so long as technology is applied for benevolent purpose – or applies itself, assuming eventual autonomous function, to such purpose – social relations are peaceable and productive. The dream of costlessness is immediately dismissed. But a Public Domain Authority could examine how technology might be applied to liberate instead of to exclude and control.

Price

Price is the greatest mystery of economic life. What price invites production and what profit margin is legitimate? No one agrees on answers to these questions. A Public Domain Authority, exempt from special pleading or interference, can suggest better answers than today's policymakers. Price demarcates market and non-market, and separates private and public. If, for example, intellectual property laws, which are the creation of more than a century of special pleading, were stripped of provisions that permit industries to engage in monopoly or maximal pricing (provisions establishing lengthy duration of monopoly, and in addition in the case of copyright, guaranteed remuneration and extensive neighbouring rights) price would drop radically.

Profit could still be made but not super-profit and the change in pricing would alter the complexion of industries and the way that society received intellectual property goods and services. Most importantly, access to these goods and services would increase and the extent of proprietary holdings would reduce, since reduction in the length of intellectual property ownership would result in the early extinguishment of otherwise long-lasting monopolies.

In other words, lower pricing, which would follow alteration to laws, would shrink the total of intellectual property holdings and deliver what was hitherto subject to ownership into the public domain. Material thus distributed would be accessible for free to anyone. Analysis of price is a fundamental prelude to creating a meaningful distributive economic policy, and a Public Doman Authority could undertake such an analysis.

When laws are denuded of provisions that entrench unfair advantage, or permit economic actors to make unfair or oppressive bargains, an entire economy changes shape, and again, the public domain increases, since the product of unfair and oppressive bargaining is the enlargement of private holdings, the concentration of wealth and the exclusion of the public.

Intellectual property

The harmful exclusionary effect of property rights in abstract subject matter and modes of distributing that subject matter is pronounced throughout the world. While we are told that these proprietary rights are necessary to preserve productive incentive and that legislative exceptions and limitations protect the public interest in access, nothing in principle justifies the application of rules against monopoly to every sector of an economy but one – that which concerns production and distribution of intellectual property material.

Allowing for the argument that monopoly rights of short duration help to protect the producer from the depredations of free-riders, the argument against free-riding is used to justify monopoly terms so lengthy that prospects of early access to material are defeated. The result is that gratuitous access to needed pharmaceuticals, or academic or educational publications, or useful information, or even entertainment content is foreclosed to those unable to pay the monopoly price.

The economic and social effect of intellectual property monopoly is thus severe: the severity of access constraint in less developed countries stymies effective knowledge dissemination and constrains the supply of necessary medicines to those who cannot afford those medicines. Open access to knowledge initiatives and other programs for encouraging dissemination, such as Creative Commons, to some extent counteract the effect of proprietary restriction. Exigency and political action have partly caused the establishment of semi-licit, or tolerated, industries manufacturing generic drugs. The problem of access in the developed world, though less acute than in less developed countries, is not fundamentally different in nature or complexion.

A Public Domain Authority could therefore usefully contribute to public debate about the scope of intellectual property rights, and their duration, with a view to advocating in the public interest for equitable limitation of the intellectual property monopoly. The public interest, in theory, lies in unrestricted access to, at the very least, useful information. If remuneration models putatively cannot accommodate early access, the nature of the models, rather than the principle should be interrogated. At any rate, by exploring questions of monopoly and access, the Public Domain Authority would fulfil an obvious need: to facilitate justifiable delivery into the public domain of material which, by exercise of proprietary rights, is withheld from early and free dissemination. Such dissemination would effect a social good without causing economic devastation to the intellectual property monopolists whose monopolies might be shortened in duration.

Information

The alternative account to that of costlessness given above argues that technology is co-opted for the purpose of control, and becomes a facilitator of wealth concentration and greater inequality. This account rejects the claim of access corporations such as Google and Facebook that they enable limitless costless information dissemination for social good. Instead, the argument is made that such access corporations facilitate and sometimes engage in information appropriation. Thus dissemination is not costless. Technology enables those who value information for diverse reasons to cost the information and pay to appropriate it.

Once appropriated, information that is not property becomes property, and information that is property becomes duplicate property. Thus technology is deployed for the purpose of appropriation and concepts of limitless and costless information are contradicted by the reality of increased ownership concentration. So too in the wider application and use of artificial intelligence and other problem-solving and distributive technologies. The dream of costlessness and social co-operation made possible by technology is revealed as a mirage.

Always, owners appropriate and always small groups control the production and use of technology. Again, questions of the social effect of the application of technology could productively be considered by a Public Domain Authority, which could contrast the potential benefits and threats of technology and suggest ways to respectively increase and mitigate potential benefit and ill-effects.

Transport

The public domain, in the sense contemplated, is more than an idea. It has been realised in town planning in different parts of the world, to some degree in planned cities like Canberra, and not least the cities of Curitiba in Brazil and Medellín in Colombia. In both instances, the municipal government, influenced by ideas and leadership of two public officials, the chief planner of Curitiba and the mayor of Medellín, chose to introduce a public domain to the urban environment. Thus, as would be commonplace in most physical public domains, which do not exist discretely but rather cohabit or co-occupy the physical environment with private and commercial property holders, they created the public amidst the private.

In practice, they dedicated public resources to creating public amenity, obeying dictates of public need rather than profit or claimed commercial necessity. Consequently, they made at least part of their cities less exclusionary. In both cases, the first element of establishing a public domain was to invest significantly in public transport systems that made speedy commuter ingress and egress a reality (Curitiba) and effectively linked slums and poorer neighbourhoods to the city centre (Medellín). An accessible and effective transport system allowed for efficient intra-city transit and made city resources accessible to hitherto deprived populations unable to gain access to those resources.

A second element of planning in these cities was to create accessible open space and provide useful social resources such as libraries. A Public Domain Authority could offer proposals on public development, suggesting strategies to make resources more accessible to people through effective town planning. Similarly, a Public Domain Authority could advise on the possibility for effective total reconfiguration of urban transport systems, giving consideration to, for instance, ubiquitous implementation of driver-less transport systems.

Conclusion

The public domain can be imagined in many more ways, and the scope of action for a Public Domain Authority is larger than the subjects of inquiry sketched above. A Public Domain Authority should be funded by government, since government is trustee for the public and custodian of the public interest. But it could equally, and perhaps more sensibly, if independence is to be preserved, be funded by continuing anonymous public donation. It could be funded by both these sources. The message remains: if the public domain is not to disappear, it must be mapped and protected. It can only be protected by a funded independent public agency such as the PDA described. It is not the enemy of the private domain but nor is it its friend. It defends itself against privatisation, and by that act creates conditions for the creation of human flourishing. The Covid-19 pandemic has shown that the erstwhile private-public social dispensation in many countries is a chimera. That is, the existence of the private is to some extent made possible by public provision and public provision can notionally be continued ad infinitum. So it was in the Roman empire and so it can be today. Public action can transform phenomena and resources in ways directed towards human flourishing precisely because what is public is not sequestered by the rules of privacy and solitary possession, and embraces what is infinite: air, space, water, sunlight, even land and certain other resources. The opposite of public action is paratrophic action, which directs benefit to the few not the many. World history is more characterised by paratrophic than public action, but public action for common good is the cause always of reduction of social inequality.

Above all, the institution of an independent Public Domain Authority in any particular jurisdiction would signify commitment to public conservation and enrichment. Private and public domains are not, or need not be, inimical. They are counter-poised but one should not diminish the other. If the public domain is to avoid its historical fate – privatisation – public action is necessary. An independent Public Domain Agency could constructively provide the intellectual and material wherewithal for such action. Enhancing the public estate, the domain of non-ownership stimulates the intercourse of ideas and the freedom to express individuality and solidarity unthreatened by enclosure.

Notes

1 The idea of eudaimonia, or living well in accordance with certain moral precepts, is attributed most commonly to Plato and Aristotle who in the Nicomachean Ethics wrote of the well-lived life of purpose.

2 See also Mark Lemley, 2004. 'Intellectual property and free-riding', *Texas Law Review* 83. Lemley argues that so-called free-riding positively increases dissemination of information for public benefit.

3 The 'tragedy of the commons' posits that public unregulated use of a resource degrades or depletes the resource because individuals do not have a private incentive to gratuitously do the work necessary to maintain the resource. Garrett Hardin coined the term in a short 1968 article – see 'The Tragedy of the Commons', *Science* 162 (3859): 1243–1248.

References

Aquinas, St Thomas. [1265–74] 1989. Summa theologiae. In: *Summa Theologiae: A Concise Translation*, trans. Timothy McDermott. Notre Dame, IN: Ave Maria Press, 1989.

Berwick, Robert and Chomsky, Noam. 2016. *Why Only Us: Language and Evolution*. Cambridge, MA: MIT Press.

Blackstone, William. [1769] 2016. *Commentaries on the Laws of England Book II*. Oxford: Oxford University Press.

Chomsky, Noam. 1957. *Syntactic Structures*. The Hague: Mouton & Co.

Chrysostom, St John. [386–98] 1950–51. 'Twelfth homily on the first epistle to St Timothy'. Bellingham, Washington: Faithlife (Logo.com). Referred to in: *The Problem of Private Property According to St. Thomas Aquinas*, eds. Hermann Chroust and Robert J. Affeldt. *Marquette Law Review*, 34(3), Winter 1950–51.

St. John Chrysostom: The prophet of charity. https://www.catholicculture.org/culture/library/view.cfm?recnum=5977.

Credit Suisse. 2012–20. *Global Wealth Report*. Zurich: Credit Suisse Research Institute at research.institute@credit-suisse.com.

Davies, James, Sandström, Susanna, Shorrocks, Anthony, Wolff, Edward. 2006–2012. *World Distribution of Household Wealth*. United Nations University-World Institute for Development Economics Research. Working Paper Series 2006–2012.

Declaration of the Rights of Man and of the Citizen. [1789] 2008. *Article 2*. Yale: Lillian Goldman Law Library (The Avalon Project).

Durkheim, Emile. [1893] 1997. *The Division of Labour in Society*. New York: Free Press.

Dworkin, Ronald. 1977. *Taking Rights Seriously*. London: Gerald Duckworth & Co.

Friedman, Milton. 1960. *A Program for Monetary Stability*. New York: Fordham University Press.

Friedman, Milton. 1962. *Capitalism and Freedom*. Chicago, IL: University of Chicago Press.

George, Henry. [1879] 2016. *Progress and Poverty: An Inquiry into the Cause of Industrial Depressions and of Increase of Want with Increase of Wealth: The Remedy*. Rookhope: Aziloth Books.

George, Henry. 1885. *The Crime of Poverty: An Address Delivered in the Opera House, Burlington, Iowa, April 1, 1885, Under the Auspices of the Burlington Assembly, no. 3135*, Knights of Labour at https://catalog.hathitrust.org/Record /006854992.

Haila, Anne. 2016. *Urban Land Rent: Singapore as a Property State*. Oxford: Wiley Blackwell.

Hayek, Friedrich. 1944. *The Road to Serfdom*. Chicago, IL: University of Chicago Press.

Hayek, Friedrich. 1960. *The Constitution of Liberty*. Oxfordshire: Routledge and Kegan Paul.

Hobbes, Thomas. [1651] 2017. *Leviathan*. London: Penguin.

Juvenal [100–127] 1967. *Satire X 16 Satires*. London: Penguin.

Keynes, John Maynard. 1936. *The General Theory of Employment, Interest and Money*. London: Palgrave Macmillan.

Kropotkin, Peter. [1892] 2015. *The Conquest of Bread*. London: Penguin.

Lammers, Joris, Galinksy, Adam, Gordijn, Ernestine and Sabine, Otten. June 2008. 'Illegitimacy moderates the effect of power on approach'. *Psychological Science*, 19(6), 558–64.

Lammers, Joris, et al. May 2012. 'Power increases social distance'. *Social Psychological and Personality Science*, 3(3), 282–90.

Lenin, Vladimir. [1921] 1965. *Collected Works*, 2nd English edition, volume 33. Moscow: Progress Publishers, 60–79.

Marx, Karl. [1873] 1992. *Capital: A Critique of Political Economy*. London: Penguin.

Marx, Karl and Engels, Friedrich. [1848] 2002. *The Communist Manifesto*. London: Penguin.

Mises, Ludwig von. [1949] 1998. *Human Action: A Treatise on Economics*. Auburn, AL: Ludwig von Mises Institute.

More, Thomas. [1516] 1967. Utopia. In: *The Essential Thomas More*, eds. James Greene and John Dolan, trans John Dolan. New York: New American Library.

Peetz, David and Murray, Georgina. 2012. 'Who owns the world? Tracing half the corporate giants' shares to 30 owners'. *The Conversation*, 12 April 2017 (discussing data published in Murray, Georgina Murray and Scott, John (eds). *Financial Elites and Transnational Business: Who Rules the World?* Cheltenham: Edward Elgar).

Piketty, Thomas. 2014. *Capital in the 21st Century*. Cambridge, MA: Harvard University Press.

Plato [c 375 BC]. 2012. *The Republic*. Trans Rowe, Christopher (2012). London: Penguin.

Plutarch [c 100–22 AD] 2005. *On Sparta*. London: Penguin.

Proudhon, Pierre-Joseph. [1840] 1994. *What is Property?* Cambridge: Cambridge University Press.

Radin, Max. 1925. 'Fundamental concepts of Roman law'. *California Law Review*, 13(3), 207–8.

Rousseau, Jean-Jacques. [1755] 1992. *Discourse on the Origin and Basis of Inequality Among Men*. Cambridge, MA: Hackett Publishing Company.

Sartre, Jean-Paul. [1943] 2020. *Being and Nothingness: An Essay on Phenomenological Ontology*. Oxford: Routledge.

Shorrocks, Anthony and Davies, James. 2018. *Comparing global inequality of income and wealth*. United Nations University-World Institute for Development Economics Research. WIDER Working Paper 2018/160, at https://www.wider.unu.edu/sites/default/files/Publications/Working-paper/PDF/wp2018-160.pdf.

Smith, Adam. [1776] 1982. *The Wealth of Nations*. London: Penguin.

Tan, Alvin. 2020. *Singapore: A Very Short History, From Temasek to Tomorrow*. Singapore: Talisman Publishing.

United Nations Development Program. 1990–2020. 'Human Development Reports', at http://hdr.undp.org/.

Veblen, Thorstein. [1899] 1994. *The Theory of the Leisure Class: An Economic Study of Institutions*. New York: Penguin, esp Chapter 9.

Walther, Nicholas. 1969. *About Anarchism (1969)*. London: Freedom Press.

World Happiness Reports. 2012–20. *Sustainable Development Solutions Network*. United Nations at https://worldhappiness.report/archive/#partners.

Zucman, Gabriel. 2017. 'Reported in Spencer Woodman "Inside the secret world of offshore mega-trusts"'. *International Consortium of Investigative Journalists*, 7 at https://www.icij.org/investigations/paradise-papers/secret-world-offshore-mega-trusts/.

Index

Note: Page numbers with "n" indicates the notes in the text.